SPAIN OBSERVED

Michèle Rodde and Michèle Affergan

Translated from the French by Stephen Hardman

KAYE & WARD · LONDON

OXFORD UNIVERSITY PRESS · NEW YORK

LEON

Las Huelga
Burgos

Peñafi

Valladolid
Coca

Segovia

Salamanca

Avila
Th

Sierra de Gredos

Toledo

LA MANCHA

CÓRDOBA

Ecija

Carmona
SEVILLE

Montefrío G

Veleta pea
Sierra Nev

Antequera

Bornos

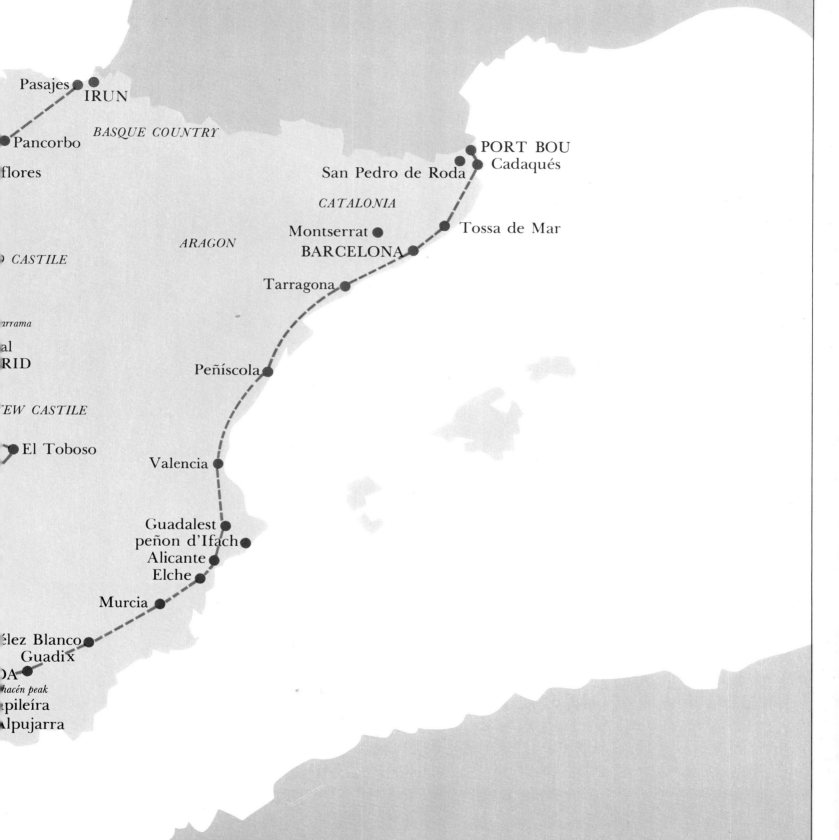

1
FROM IRÚN TO MADRID

The village of Pancorbo

There is the Spain of the atlas and the text-book; there is also the Spain of the poet and the traveller. It is certainly not the authors' intention to set one against the other, for a visual and aesthetic knowledge of a country is as necessary for its appreciation as a knowledge of its geography, its economy or its history. The purpose of this book is not to relate the story of Spain, but to let the reader see the country for himself, or at least to see its most striking aspects. It is hoped that the photographs which accompany this text will reveal some of the secrets of Spain's magnificent past. In presenting these photographs the authors have reluctantly been obliged to select, in other words to eliminate. Moreover, the most powerful emotions are not always aroused by the most well-known buildings or views: sometimes a photograph of an unfamiliar place can be richer in emotion and more stimulating than the most famous landscapes or creations of man.

As soon as the traveller approaching Spain from France crosses the frontier and arrives in Irún, he is tempted to ask himself where the real Spain begins, the Spain evoked by the richly coloured images of Victor Hugo, Théophile Gautier and Prosper Mérimée, that outpost of Africa in the south of the European Continent. For, at first, there is no marked difference between the countryside which he has just left behind and that which he now sees around him.

Arid, sun-scorched Spain, the soul-stirring Spain which still bears the traces of nearly eight centuries of Muslim presence, does not immediately show herself to the impatient traveller. First he must cross several barriers, the first of which, along the road from Irún to Madrid, is the **gorge of Pancorbo**, a natural rampart rising between the green mountains of the Basque Country and the vast ochre horizon of Old Castile. The menacing shapes of the enormous rocks seem to be defending the passage hollowed out by a little torrent. The **village of**

4   The gorge of Pancorbo

Pancorbo, at the foot of this forbidding 'fortress', has lost much of its past glory; only the ruins of two castles bear witness to the strategic role that it once played. The first, Santa María, built by the Moors, is a relic of the battles of the Reconquest. The second, Santa Engracia, built in 1794, reminds the visitor that Pancorbo was the scene of a battle between the French army and Spain's ally, the Duke of Wellington, during the War of Independence against Napoleon; the castle was razed by the French in 1823, during the expedition led by the Duke of Angoulême.

This first encounter with Spain is also a first encounter with Spanish history. It will not be the last, for the country's turbulent past is in evidence almost at every step.

Since Irún the traveller has been passing through the Spanish **Basque Country**. Around him he will have heard the people speaking Castilian – in other words, Spanish, a Latin language like French. Soon, even the visitor who does not understand Spanish will distinguish harsher sounds belonging to a mysterious language, Basque, the origins of which are lost in the obscurity of time.

French historian, Jules Michelet, wrote: 'The Basque, immutable, has seen every nation pass before him: Carthaginians, Celts, Romans, Goths and Saracens. He looks with pity on our young antiquities. A Montmorency said to one of them:

'"Do you know that we are a thousand years old?"

'"And we," said the Basque, "no longer count how old we are."'

Is it possible that this peaceful land, these misty valleys in which lie dainty villages, these delightful little forts, such as Ondarroa and **Pasajes**, should have witnessed so many invasions and yet the Basque people should still have preserved its language and personality intact? Is it possible that the mighty and long-established process of industrialization – at Bilbao, for example – should not have tainted the distinctive traits of the Basque character? One has only to see a Basque festival to be reassured that this colourful folklore, with its dances performed to the shrill music of the *xistu*, is still very much alive. While they love to sing, dance and drink, the Basques also have the

Pasajes

ruggedness and pride of an isolated people ready to face the perils of the sea, the independence and strength of character of mountain-dwellers; they are fishermen and shepherds, but also adventurers who set off to try their luck all over the world, smugglers whose way of life is typified by the figure of Ramuntcho and who obey no law but their own. These are romantic images, perhaps, but beyond these images one discovers the warrior Basque, courageous and enamoured of liberty, who wishes to be neither Spanish nor French, but above all Basque. And the countryside, which presents the same graceful features on both banks of the Bidassoa, seems to justify his pride.

'Castile cannot see the sea', writes Azorín, one of the authors who, at the beginning of this century, rediscovered the Castilian values of endurance, steadfastness and honour. Miguel de Unamuno, a Basque, seems to reply to Azorín, a native of eastern Spain, that Castile is indeed 'a petrified sea filled with sky'. In a poem of an almost mystical fervour, Unamuno evokes this land which finds its only outlet in the sky and in the values of the spirit:

> You uplift me, land of Castile,
> In the gnarled palm of your hand,
> To the sky which inspires and refreshes you.
> To the sky, your master.

The façade of the cathedral

In the distance **Burgos** appears, the ash-grey halo which surrounds it broken by the pink patches of the roofs of Roman tiles. Above the compact town rises the imposing mass of the cathedral, elegant and youthful despite its 750 years. Théophile Gautier has left an evocative description of the **cathedral** of Burgos, with its two spires 'chiselled in the tiniest details like the setting of a ring. . . . It is a whirl of sculptures, arabesques, statues, colonnettes, mouldings, lancet arches and pendentives which are enough to give you vertigo.' The visitor also feels romantic stirrings in his soul as he contemplates this enormous jewel, uplifting, slightly wild and sometimes a little grandiose, on which German, Burgundian and Spanish architects collaborated from the thirteenth to the sixteenth centuries.

Before entering the cathedral, you should first go round the outside, starting from the right or south side (thus you will be able to follow the history of the cathedral). First, on the Calle de la Paloma, you come to the Puerta del Sarmental, part of the original thirteenth-century building, in a French style. You then pass along the fourteenth-century cloister. The chapels of the apse date from the fifteenth and sixteenth centuries. From the top of Calle Fernán González there is a fine view of the **Chapel of the Condestable**, built at the end of the fifteenth century, in the flowery ogival style, at the command of the Condestable of Castile, Pedro Hernández de Velasco; from the same viewpoint you can also see the lantern-turret and one of the spires.

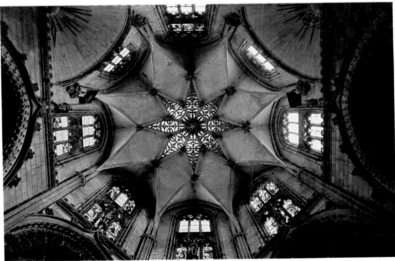
The Chapel of the Condestable

Opposite the Puerta del Sarmental is the Puerta Alta with thirteenth-century statues; the Puerta de la Pellejería, close by but on a lower level, displays the exuberance of the later Plateresque style (so named because it resembles the work of the *platero* or goldsmith).

The **façade**, unfortunately altered in the eighteenth century, has lost most of the sculptures on the Santa María doorway, but it still has a proud dignity with its twin spires and its windows. Inside, you can admire the

dome, an astounding feat of lightness and elegance, rising some fifty metres above the transept; the cathedral contains innumerable curiosities, works of art and treasures.

Old Castile, the crucible of Spain's whole national history, is an austere region, tempered like steel; its importance dates from the early tenth century and the decisive moments of the first stage of the Reconquest. It is in Castile that the heart of Spain still beats today. Rarely has the aspect of a countryside coincided so closely with the epic history of a nation; rarely have the visible virtues of a countryside played such a large part in fashioning the hearts of men. The high Castilian plain or *Meseta* is elevated not only in altitude, but also in the human aspirations and ideals which it has aroused over the centuries. In the eleventh century, across this endless heathland where the tender green of the springtime turns brutally to yellow and then to the colour of burnt bread in the full heat of the summer, this poor ground traditionally devoted to corn and sheep, rode El Cid and his troops in the impalpable dust of wind and dry soil.

In the environs of Burgos other artistic marvels await the traveller – the monasteries. There are two situated along the perimeter of the town, a mile or two from the centre: the *cartuja* (Carthusian monastery) of Miraflores and the Abbey of Las Huelgas. It is well worth walking for at least the last part of the route leading to the **Carthusian monastery of Miraflores**, for this building stands in a privileged position at the top of a hill and amid perfect calm; at the top of the gentle slope you will be able to observe the beauty of the monastery, built in a quietly refined Gothic style. The cloister, white and luminous, gives the same impression of peace. The church, also Gothic, contains some remarkable sculptures by the artist, Gil de Siloé, who seems almost to have given life to his figures of white marble and alabaster on the tombs of Juan II, his wife and the Infante Alfonso.

The **abbey of Las Huelgas** is older, dating from the late twelfth century. You should give yourself time to make a thorough tour of the interior of the monastery, where many relics of the Middle Ages are preserved, including fabrics and clothing found in the tombs and the Moorish standard captured by the Spanish at the celebrated battle of Las Navas de Tolosa (1212). There is also a magnificent series of sixteenth-century tapestries.

The monastery of Santo Domingo de Silos is not on the road from Burgos to Madrid, but is worth a little detour to the east, for it possesses the most beautiful Romanesque cloister in the region, with twin columns and justly famous capitals.

The cloister of the monastery of Miraflores

A tapestry in the monastery of Las Huelgas (*top*)

Detail from the doorway of the monastery of Miraflores

Castile (Castilla in Spanish) is well named, for it is the country of castles (*castillos*). In the distance, on the plain, the famous castles described by Ortega y Gasset as 'hungry warriors' rise up like rocks, haughty and impregnable; this writer, better known as a philosopher, evokes magnificently 'the eloquent gesticulation of the ruins . . . these warlike castles which, with the toothless jaws of their battlements, bite the blue of the sky'.

To make a tour of the castles of Castile is to go back through the centuries to the time when Christian Spain was beginning to establish her identity in the struggle against the Muslim invader. The conquest had been com-

The castle of Coca

pleted swiftly: within two years the Arabs had occupied the entire peninsula, except for Asturias where the Christian warriors took refuge under their leader Pelayo. The Reconquest was a slow advance southwards which began on the arrival of the Arabs in 711 and lasted until 1492. But the war was not fought continuously for 800 years. Muslim Spain was tolerant; on each side of a constantly moving frontier, the religion, language and laws of both Spaniards and Muslims were respected, with all the interacting influences which such a co-existence involved. The period of the Reconquest has left traces of a civilization unique in history.

The castles of Castile were built from the tenth century onwards to defend the frontier of the Duero-Christians to the north, Arabs to the south. They are to be found everywhere, with their sonorous names and glorious walls – Fuensaldaña, Torrelobatón, Mota del Marqués, Villalba de los Albores. The castle of **Coca** is one of the most beautiful and well preserved. **Peñafiel**, with its formidable enclosure-wall twenty-three metres in width, resembles a gigantic ship stranded in the plain.

Preceding pages: a scene
Old Castile in the region
Tierra de Campos

14

The castle of Peñafiel

Valladolid, a typically Castilian city, where the purest Spanish of the whole peninsula is spoken (according to the Spaniards of the other regions), has the slightly antiquated charm and tranquillity of an old provincial town.

As the capital, under Philip II and Philip III, of an immense empire that embraced a large part of Europe and also the recently conquered New World, another empire on which 'the sun never set', Valladolid witnessed all the splendour of the Spanish court. Once the capital of a kingdom, Valladolid has been able to adapt itself to the role of a lively commercial and provincial capital and the visitor will find here all the bustle of a modern city.

The most famous buildings in Valladolid are undoubtedly the church of San Pablo and the **Colegio San**

Valladolid — the patio of the Colegio San Gregorio

Gregorio, which stand a few yards from one another and form a harmonious architectural ensemble; both edifices date from the fifteenth century, the period of the unification of Spain, and their façades are in the same style, an accumulation of detail arranged in a symphony of stone.

Passing through the doorway of San Gregorio, you come into a *patio*, or courtyard, with intricately worked balustrades in which profusion borders on excess without ever becoming excessive – an artistry by which light is endlessly fragmented and reflected. The college accommodates the National Museum of Sculpture, the largest collection of Castilian polychrome statuary, including sculptures by Berruguete, Juan de Juni and Gregorio Fernández. One room is devoted to the famous *pasos* or scenes from the Passion, in which realism and pathos are equally powerful. During Holy Week the *pasos* are carried ceremoniously in the processions organized by the numerous religious brotherhoods of the city, each of which has its own costumes and liturgical ornaments. The **Palm Sunday procession** makes its way through the whole city, bearing long palms with entrancing effect.

The best time to visit Valladolid is during Holy Week. The only problem is the difficulty of finding accommodation at this season of the year. A friend of the authors related how, on her last visit to the city, having failed to find a hotel room, she sought refuge in a religious institution where the mother superior only agreed to offer her a roof after careful reflection, obviously suspecting that it was not faith alone that had brought her to Valladolid.

Valladolid – the Palm Sunday procession

Whether you approach it from Valladolid, from Portugal or from Andalusia, you should make sure of reaching **Salamanca** just as the sun is sinking, when the city begins to glow in a dazzling mass of towers, domes and steeples, acquiring a dual identity as its gilded buildings are outlined against the cloudless sky and reflected in the waters of the Río Tormes. From the opposite bank of the river, which is spanned by a Roman bridge of powerful proportions, one has an unforgettable vision of the city so appropriately known as 'Little Rome'. Even before entering Salamanca, the traveller is already convinced by its exterior aspect that this city has achieved a balance between the joys of the spirit and the refined pleasures of the senses.

The most enchanting feature of Salamanca is the ochre colouring of the stone, a soft stone which, as it becomes oxidized, assumes a warm old-gold hue. 'It is a feast for the eyes and for the spirit to see the city set its gold against the silver of the sky, to see it reflected in the waters of the Tormes, assuming a double existence and resembling a frieze suspended in space.' (Unamuno)

Above the modest tiers of houses – Salamanca is built on three hills – rises the imposing mass of the cathedrals, the old and the new, the monastery of San Esteban and, behind, the Clerecía, once a Jesuit house; the towers and steeples that spring up from these buildings seem almost to pierce the sky.

As you walk through the city you will find near the Clerecía a fine civic edifice dating from the time of the 'Catholic Kings', the **Casa de las Conchas** (House of the Shells). It owes its name to the scallop shells arranged in quincunxes across the entire façade. The *concha* was the emblem of the pilgrims who visited the shrine of St James of Compostela

Salamanca – the Casa de las Conchas

in Galicia. Other buildings, such as the Monterrey palace and the Casa de las Duenas, belong to the same period.

What would Salamanca be without its **university**? In the fourteenth century Salamanca was one of the greatest universities in Europe, the equal of Oxford, Paris and Bologna. It reached its zenith in the sixteenth century, the Spanish Golden Age when the arts and literature enjoyed a mighty upsurge. Young nobles came here to study the humanities and were followed by their servants, who were also students as can be seen in Spanish picaresque novels. Nowadays, there are only four faculties – literature, law, sciences and medicine – but student activity is still very much in evidence, in the patios where the students stroll or in front of the university when the **tuna**, a colourful student orchestra, comes to play and sing for the enjoyment of all.

As you walk along Calle Calderón de la Barca and into the Patio de las Escuelas, you find yourself immediately plunged into the very heart of Salamancan art. Three miracles of the Spanish Renaissance stand in close proximity: the doorway of the Hospital del Estudio; the doorway and patio of Las Escuelas Menores; and the façade of the university itself, a perfect example of Plateresque art.

Of the Patio de las Escuelas Menores, Miguel de Unamuno, a spiritual son of Salamanca and for several years the rector of the university, says with emotion: 'Not for anything in the world would I exchange this patio, filled in its silence with the murmurs of the centuries, this patio sheltered from the din of trams, railways and futile human agitation.'

All the great intellects of the Golden Age passed through the university of Salamanca. The presence of the humanist Fray Luis de León is felt everywhere; his statue, the arm held

out in a gesture of peace, guards the entrance. The guide will not omit to tell you how Fray Luis de León, condemned as a free-thinker by the Inquisition, was imprisoned in 1572 and how in 1576, when he resumed his lectures in the same hall, he uttered the famous words: 'We were saying yesterday. . . .'

The *tuna*, a student orchestra

Salamanca – the patio of the university

As you leave the university, Salamanca unfolds before you. If you find yourself hesitating between the need for relaxation and a visit to the **cathedral** close by, why not combine pleasure with architectural beauty by going to the **Plaza Mayor**, about which you will already have heard so much? Resolving to come back to the cathedral shortly, you can take Calle Mayor which leads to the famous square.

As you come on to the Plaza Mayor, you will doubtless be struck by the elegance of its square form; arcades enhance and give air to what might otherwise have been mere heaviness. This vast architectural ensemble, begun in 1729, was completed in 1755 in the reign of Philip V, the first Bourbon king of Spain. Above the arcades of the ground-floor rise three storeys crowned by a graceful balustrade. Until the middle of the nineteenth century bullfights (*corridas*) took place on the square, which is still the hub of the city's life.

Stop at one of the multicoloured café terraces which jut out informally on to the square, and settle yourself at a table, amidst the hum of conversation and the coming and going of the crowds under the arcades. The waiter (*camarero*) will be ready for any linguistic effort required of him by foreign customers. He will offer you a varied menu, perhaps too varied; if in doubt, try some delicious *gambas a la plancha* (grilled prawns) and a few local dainties such as *yemas* and *mazapán*.

After a little rest and refreshment you can return to the cathedral. On the way you will be able to have another look at the Casa de las Conchas and the Clerecía, built by the Jesuits; the courtyard of the Clerecía (the seat of the Pontifical University) is a composition of Baroque masses, gigantic and yet refined.

In fact, Salamanca has two cathedrals in one. The old cathedral (Catedral Vieja) dates from the twelfth century and has a remarkable Mudejar tower called the Torre del Gallo (Tower of the Cock). Embedded in the masonry of the new cathedral (Catedral Nueva), the old building seems to be huddling against it. In its architectural simplicity the Catedral Vieja is a marvel of the Romanesque style, with an apse and an octagonal tower which set the seal on its nobility. It is a pity that, in the construction of the new cathedral, the old building lost the north arm of its transept. The construction of the Catedral Nueva, begun under Ferdinand the Catholic, continued for two centuries and, as often happens in Spain, its architecture presents a succession of different styles: Gothic, Renaissance and Baroque. Unity is achieved by the colour and texture of the stone.

Salamanca — the Plaza Mayor

Salamanca — the cathedral

Melons ripening in the sun

is commonly supposed to be the personification of sanity, also engulfed in Don Quixote's madness?

The **sheep** of Castile are very real. Through the ages the Castilian peasant has eaten them and woven their wool. The culinary ingenuity of this poor region has invented the *cordero asado*, lamb baked in the oven or on a spit, golden brown and succulent, a real delight to the palate, especially if washed down with one of the sparkling local wines.

It is an old custom of the Castilian countryside to preserve a food rare in winter, **melons** which have previously been ripened on straw, under a bed or in a cellar, and which are eaten on Christmas Eve.

'I understand why these fields have produced souls enamoured of the ideal. . . . Souls thirsting for a super-human ideal, detached from this sad life, full of the dryness of this soil and the heat of this sky, eager for a justice as pure as the sun, for an infinite glory. . . . These expanses inspired Cervantes; here, one understands the secret spirit of an epic so sad that it made the humorist Heine weep, this poem in which reality and life seem so small, and madness and death so great. . . .'

This mystical vision which Unamuno, the author of *Del Sentimiento trágico de la vida* ('The Tragic Sense of Life'), gives of a Castile that caused Don Quixote to lose his reason should not make one forget the other face of Castile, the Castile which gave birth to Sancho Panza. The Castilian is certainly tragic and austere, but he is also *socarrón* ('crafty' is an approximation to the meaning of the Spanish word), cheerful and affable. The Don Quixote-Sancho Panza dualism expresses all the ambivalence of the peasant who has his feet on the ground – even in the ground – and whose meditative self tends to look upwards to the sky. In Cervantes' novel there is contamination between the two characters and the more foolish of the two is not always Don Quixote. How easily does the worthy Sancho allow himself to be persuaded by his master that the peaceful herds of sheep are the armies of the Giant and have come to put them to the test! Is not the mirage shared by both men? But reality regains the upper hand when the valorous Don Quixote, prompt to attack, finds that his adversaries are only shepherds who are terrified by this ranting madman and who defend themselves victoriously with slings. Was not Sancho, who

Next page:
Old Castile — the threshing of the corn or *trilla*

Old Castile — a herd of sheep

Avila — the cathedral

As the traveller penetrates into the heart of Castile he sees, to the west, the majestic profile of the Sierra de Gredos. Suddenly, perched on the top of a hill, appears the huge fortified city of **Avila**, its **walls** intact and seemingly impenetrable. The *muralla* follows every variation in the level of the terrain, every fold of the rock, leaving no gap. Impassive, remote from the world, its only dialogue is with the light. The entire city still lies within the mighty barrier of its walls. Placed under their protection, withdrawing into itself and insensible to the assaults of modern life, it asserts itself, Catholic and provincial.

The **cathedral**, enclosed by the wall, seems to belong to the fortifications. 'With its battlements and parapet-walks, its covered gallery and its parade-ground, the cathedral is a warlike edifice, very Catholic but hardly Christian,' writes Camilo José Cela who, thinking of the Inquisition, adds: 'this cathedral hardly helps us to realize that the Jew who was burnt at the stake may also have had a soul. . . .'

This cathedral-fortress was built in the twelfth century and altered in the eighteenth. The interior is narrow and has a sober strength that contrasts with a delicate Renaissance ornamentation. The retable behind the high altar was partly executed by Pedro Berruguete, whose *Life of St Thomas* can be seen in the monastery of Santo Tomás.

Avila is a *mystical* city. A woman, St Theresa, imbues the city with her spirituality. Teresa de Cepeda de Ahumada is one of Spain's great figures. As a child she dreamed with her brother of offering herself for martyrdom at the hands of the Infidels. As a woman she channelled her bubbling energy into a zealous activity that convulsed the Carmelite order. Disgusted by the relaxations that were adulterating monastic and convent life, Teresa wanted to be a reformer and to rediscover the purity and rigour of earlier days.

Her mystical revelation of 1558 created a yearning for perfection and took her across the whole of Castile. 'This struggle in which St Theresa engaged was not only against men. The obstacles of nature, the rigours of the climate, illness and bad weather must have tested her no less severely. Strange adventures, indeed, which in many cases can only be compared with the vicissitudes of a picaresque novel.' (Pierre Lafue)

This enclosed city offers the visitor not only its monuments, its altar-pieces, its tombs and the memory of St Theresa. The authors have stood dreaming in its lanes and its cosy inns have welcomed them. But did they tame Avila, or did Avila tame them?

Avila — a view of the city

Segovia — the aqueduct

In direct contrast to Avila, a city shut off from the world, **Segovia** offers itself to the visitor, smiling sweetly like a city of the Florentine countryside. It is built on a rocky spur between two deep valleys and stands out against the snow-capped peaks of the Sierra de Guadarrama, like a slender ship with the Alcázar as the figure on its prow. Before going into the city, pause awhile to contemplate the poplars mingling with the spires of the Alcázar, the pinnacles of the cathedral, the delicate steeples of the churches, and the towers of the palaces, in a light of extraordinary transparency.

The **aqueduct**, the symbol of Segovia's ancient origins, seems to be watching over the city which, at certain times of the day, it covers with the huge shadows of its arches. Standing witness to the city's prosperity at the time of the Roman colonization, the aqueduct has survived the centuries and the robustness of its 118 arches, spanning a distance of 728 metres, appears unshakeable. This colossal structure, which still distributes water, depends for its stability solely on the weight of its granite blocks.

Having enjoyed great prestige in the Roman period, Segovia had to wait until the fifteenth century to regain its importance. It was here that Isabella the Catholic was proclaimed queen of Castile in 1474. Originally an Arab construction, the **Alcázar** underwent renovation and embellishment in the fourteenth and early fifteenth centuries. After visiting the Alcázar, you can venture as far as the Paseo de los Reyes, a level stretch at the end of the rocky spur. But the image of the Alcázar that one remembers most vividly is its romantic silhouette, powerful and at the same time delicate, which under a stormy sky calls to mind the fantastic castles that haunt the imagination in childhood.

Segovia — the Alcázar

Segovia – the cathedral

The streets of Segovia are lively and colourful. As you stroll along them at random, you will come across many small Romanesque churches. The high six-storey tower of San Esteban, surmounted by a pointed belfry, has been called 'the queen of Spanish towers'. Not far away stands the **cathedral**, in the Late Gothic style. Elegant and yet sober, imposing and yet light, built in a warm stone, 'the Lady of cathedrals' raises skywards its clusters of buttresses surmounted by ornate pinnacles. It is certainly beautiful and pure in style, and the Plaza Mayor adjoining its apse has all the charm of a Spanish square. Yet nothing can equal the aesthetic pleasure given by a masterpiece of Romanesque art such as the church of San Millán, which lies outside the city walls. One cannot fail to admire the assurance of its forms, which suddenly achieve lightness in a marvellous exterior portico.

Returning along Avenida Fernández towards the Plaza Azoguejo and then along Calle Cervantes, you come to the curious **Casa de los Picos** (House of the Peaks), reminiscent of the Casa de las Conchas in Salamanca. Camilo José Cela offers various explanations of the origin of the *picos*: 'Opinions differ as to the rightness or wrongness of the *picos*: for some, this façade shows a certain Italianate style; the Marquis of Lozoya thinks that it belongs to the Isabelline style; the people choose to attribute it to the owner's desire to efface the name of House of the Jew which it bore in earlier times, and the urchins of Segovia – for everyone considers his own interests – insist that it is only there to prevent them from playing with their balloons.'

You should not leave Segovia without going to one of its typical inns: the *cochinillo asado* (roast sucking-pig) is in itself worth the effort. If you feel in the mood, you will find all kinds of other specialities – roast lamb, Villacastín trout, *yemas*, etc. – for this city of artistic treasures is also a city of good food and wine.

Segovia – the Casa de los Picos

The Escorial

The Escorial — the façade

'Philip's eyes, the colour of ash, measured the abyss of loneliness that stretched between his empire and his own person, between Cartagena of the Indies and St Lawrence of the Escorial. Like the spider, the Escorial spread its threads, quivering under the terror of the Inquisition, to every corner of the empire.'

Erected on an expanse of volcanic scoriae from which its name derives, the **Escorial** is monastery, palace and royal pantheon all in one – grey and cold, a strange sight in this bare countryside, as if planted here at the whim of a demented creator.

Philip II himself laid the first stone of the building in 1563. The Escorial owes its existence to a vow made by the monarch. In the battle of Saint-Quentin, in which the French were defeated by Spain, artillery fire had destroyed a monastery dedicated to St Lawrence. To atone for this sacrilege, and also to give his father, Charles V, a worthy burial-place, Philip II decided to erect this monumental edifice.

Work on the building took twenty-five years. For the architects, Juan Bautista de Toledo, who worked with Michelangelo on St Peter's in Rome, and Juan de Herrera, the task was, to say the least, unusual. Philip, seated on a rock ('la Silla del Rey') overlooking the site, himself made corrections and suggestions, supervising the work in its tiniest details and thus making the Escorial a truly personal achievement.

A sort of Spanish Vatican, the edifice forms an enormous quadrilateral and is said to have been designed in imitation of a gigantic gridiron in commemoration of the torture of St Lawrence. Symmetrical, without ornament, icily severe and lacking the grace of contemporary French and Italian monuments, the Escorial gives an impression of extravagance which betrays the mentality of the Spain of this period – or, at least, that of its sovereign.

Philip II, the incarnation of sadness and severity, governed an immense empire from his study. His royal bedroom was a monk's cell. He indulged a morbid religiosity and it is said that he used to sleep in his coffin in order to live his death more vividly. From the window of this room, which communicates with the church, the king followed every religious service until his dying hour.

The palace was also a royal pantheon and so, to justify its existence, the king had the coffins of kings and queens brought from all parts of Spain. One day, beneath a leaden sky, Don Quixote encountered one of these strange funeral processions in the course of his wanderings across Castile – fact and fiction briefly coinciding.

The immensity of the Sierra de Guadarrama, the vastness of the Escorial, the greatness of Spain.

But the stage was set for decline: the Arabs and Jews, who represented one-fifth of the population and formed the backbone of the country's economy, were expelled. Monks, hidalgos and rogue soldiers (*pícaros*) constituted a large and unproductive social group. The rural areas were abandoned. The gold from the Americas had become a mere dream. Monarchs were praying.

The Sierra de Guadarrama

2

MADRID

Madrid – the Retiro park

'Tres meses de invierno, nueves meses de infierno' ('three months of winter, nine months of hell'), say the Spaniards. In case you are wondering what kind of 'hell' Madrid has to offer, they only mean the climate.

Madrid, made the capital of Spain by Philip II, has taken a long time to establish itself as a rival of the great European capitals. Even ten years ago, the rhythm of the city's life was still that of a provincial town. Time was allowed to flow by and this aspect of the capital has not totally disappeared: Madrid and its parks and promenades invite the visitor to stroll at his ease and to forget the summer days of 'hell'.

In the evenings the people of Madrid go to the Paseo del Prado, the Paseo de Recoletos or the Paseo de la Castellana to seek a breath of air, or linger over refreshments in the parks. On Sundays they gather in the **Retiro Park**, an island of greenery in the city-centre. At such times it is difficult to imagine that Madrid lies at the heart of the most barren and severe region of Spain, the central Meseta. This fact seems even more unreal when one discovers the great expanse of water in this park, once called 'Buen Retiro', where Philip II used to give lavish entertainments on boats. But the twentieth century has asserted itself amid the fountains and gardens of the past. Another Madrid has risen up, now assuming an American atmosphere and, on the **Plaza de España**, boasting the two highest skyscrapers in Europe. This is an astonishing metamorphosis for a city that was only a township at the time when Salamanca, Avila and Valladolid were dazzling capitals. Madrid served as a stronghold during the Reconquest and in the fourteenth century sometimes received the Cortes (the parliamentary assemblies of Spain). Passing sovereigns stayed at the Alcázar. When Philip II decided to make it the first city of his empire, he was doubtless attracted by the solitude of its setting, but also by its situation at the geographical centre of Spain. The new capital rapidly asserted its own architectural personality. The architecture of the Escorial set the fashion and

Madrid – the Plaza de España

under Philip III and Philip IV gave rise to the characteristic Madrid style: long, bare façades in the manner of Herrera, sober towers and Flemish pinnacles. Since that time Madrid has been given the spaces, public buildings and palaces due to its rank.

A tour of Madrid can be divided into historical zones so that the visitor can see the different faces of Madrid in turn: medieval Madrid, the Madrid of the House of Austria, the Madrid of the Bourbons and of Goya, and nineteenth-century Madrid, the hub of Spain's political life. It was in the capital that the War of Independence against the Napoleonic invasion began on 2 May 1808, and it was there that the Republic was enthusiastically proclaimed on 14 April 1931. Five years later, during the Spanish Civil War, Madrid became the seat of the Republican government.

You approach the modern city along the Gran Vía, one of the main thoroughfares, crammed with cars and people

Madrid – the Plaza de España

Madrid – the Plaza de Cibeles

as is only to be expected. With Calle de Alcala, which runs parallel and leads to the Puerta del Sol, the Gran Vía encloses the commercial and business district: banks, large cafés, clubs reserved for men, more recent cafeterias, cinemas, theatres, big stores and luxury shops – all are to be found here. The tourist will inevitably be drawn by the shop-windows and will probably want to buy some buckskin clothes or shoes at tempting prices.

From the **Plaza de Cibeles** where the pretentious Post Office building stands (mockingly known as 'Our Lady of the Post' by the people of Madrid), you take the Gran Vía which brings you into the Plaza de España. From the top of a skyscraper the whole of Madrid is visible with its chaotic districts, its intercrossing streets, its towers and pinnacles, and the groups of bronze figures balancing like tight-rope walkers on the roof-tops. The capital has not escaped the virus of the 'mushroom city' and the new suburbs being built to accommodate an ever-increasing working population are encroaching further and further on to the Castilian plain, enclosed by the Sierra de Guadarrama.

Although Madrid has now attained the rank of a modern city, it is possible to forget the noise and the huge blocks of buildings, for the sky is always there. In all the main squares a haven of freshness awaits the visitor, with **fountains** playing in the **Plaza de España**, the Plaza de Cibeles, the Plaza de Neptuno and the Plaza de Apolo. Near the Plaza de España lie the Sabatini gardens, the Campo del Moro, the Royal Palace and the Plaza de Oriente, forming a particularly impressive ensemble, a perfect summer residence bathed in greenery. The Royal Palace is undoubtedly the most sumptuous example of the Neo-Classical architecture of Madrid. Between 1738 and

Madrid – the Retiro park

1764, Philip V and Charles III sank a fortune in its construction; the edifice, designed by the architects Sachetti and Ventura Rodríguez, was built in pink Guadarrama granite and Colmenar limestone. The visitor can admire the great staircase of black and white marble, one of the palace's most beautiful adornments, the royal apartments, the room of porcelains (in a frenzied Rococo style) and, above all, the superb collection of tapestries, mostly Flemish and Spanish.

On leaving the palace you can go along Calle Mayor, which leads to the historic heart of the capital, the Puerta del Sol, still just as it is described in Spanish novels of the nineteenth century. From the bell-tower of the Gobernación, the most popular clock in Madrid chimes in its grave and marvellously pure tones. This clock gives the time to the whole of Spain; on the evening of the feast of

St Sylvester, following an old custom, people come here to listen to the twelve strokes of midnight, eating twelve grapes one by one as the clock chimes.

If Madrid is not a city of ancient architecture, it is certainly a city of museums. The **Prado** alone makes the journey to the capital worthwhile. The sovereigns of Spain, enlightened patrons of the arts, acquired the works of the most celebrated artists. Spanish painting is itself admirably represented in its continuity. Nearly all the canvases of Velázquez are to be found at the Prado; a small room is devoted to his masterpiece, **Las Meninas** (*The Maids of Honour*), in which the Infanta Margarita is seen surrounded by her two *meninas* (maids of honour) and two dwarfs, with the painter himself standing in front of his easel, painting the king and queen, whose reflections can be seen in the mirror at the back of the room.

The attention of every figure in this picture is directed to another scene. 'The whole painting observes a scene for which, in turn, there exists another scene', writes Michel Foucault in a masterly analysis of *Las Meninas*. 'A first glance at the picture reveals the object of attention – the sovereigns. Their presence is divined in the respectful looks of the figures, in the surprise of the child and the dwarfs. They can be observed in the centre of the painting, in the two little silhouettes reflected in the mirror. . . . They arrange the entire composition round themselves; it is towards them that the figures face, towards them that they turn, and for their eyes that the princess is presented in her party dress.'

The wonderful gallery of portraits left by El Greco gives one the feeling of gaining a deeper knowledge of the mystical Catholic Spain of the Golden Age. Those ascetic faces, with their high, bulging brows and feverish eyes, are the contemporaries of St Theresa and St John of the Cross. The **Caballero de la mano en el pecho** (*Nobleman with Hand on Breast*) seems to be swearing on his honour that he has never failed in his duty to God, to the king, or to his own name.

The **Santa Casilda** by Zurbarán suggests the aloof, aristocratic attitude of a great lady of the seventeenth

The Prado – *Caballero de la mano en el pecho* by El Greco

The Prado – *Las Meninas* by Velázquez

The Prado – *Santa Casilda* by Zurbarán

century. The virtuosity in the treatment of the fabrics makes this painting an astounding feat of artistic bravura.

Hieronymus Bosch appealed so strongly to Philip II because he offered meditations on religion, life and death. In the seventeenth century he was one of the artists who had the audacity 'to paint man as he is within' (Guevara). Nowadays he is regarded either as a surrealist, a painter of the repressed desires of mankind, or as a mystic fascinated by the esoteric. Endowed with a prolific imagination, Hieronymus Bosch expressed in a strange symbolical form themes centred on the Christian life, on sin and redemption. The triptych known as *The Garden of Delights*, his masterpiece, represents the Garden of Eden in the right panel and Hell in the left panel. Interpretations of the central section differ: some see it as an allegory of the curse of the flesh, while for others it is the expression of a serene and chaste sexuality with all the innocence of the vegetable kingdom.

At a distance of three centuries, Goya is seen to have been another visionary moralist. His etchings – *The Disasters of War*, *Tauromachy* and *Caprices* – are a pitilessly mocking pageant of the ugliness of the world and of the phantasmagorias that inhabit the artist's imagination (and ours). The painting of **May 3 1808** depicts the executions that took place in Madrid on the day after the uprising of 2 May against the French occupying forces, a revolt which unleashed the War of Independence. It is a scene of horror and protest, a militant painting. Before the anonymous mass standing in line, before the human machine which kills, stands the hero of independence, the spirit of struggle, who is both individual and people.

If one compares the details of these two paintings (*opposite*, *right*), one discovers the same attitude of the crucified figure, the same expression of anguish; but, unlike the world of Bosch, that of Goya is a world without God. Man is now struggling against man and for man.

The Prado – *May 3 1808* by Goya

The Prado –
The Garden of Delights
by Hieronymus Bosch.
Detail: 'The Kingdom of the Millennium'

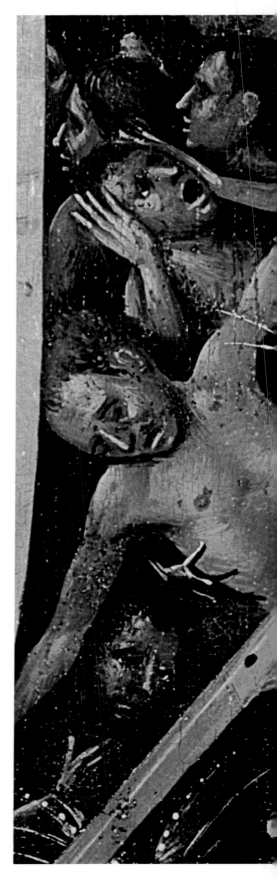

The Prado –
The Garden of Delights
by Hieronymus Bosch.
Detail: 'Hell'

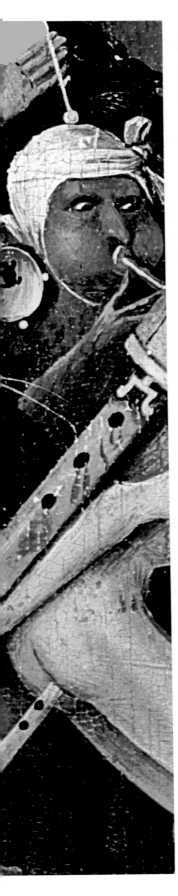

May 3 1808 by Goya. Detail

The old Madrid is the city of the *rufianes* of the Golden Age, the medieval city with its poor, its beggars and its miracle-workers, the world of the heroes of Galdós, the Spanish Balzac. One enters the old quarter by the Plaza de la Villa. Opposite the church of San Nicolás de los Servitas, the oldest in Madrid, stands the Torre de los Lujanes where the arrogant Charles V imprisoned Francis I after the battle of Pavia. Calle del Sacramento and Calle del Nuncio lead to the church of San Pedro, and the entrancing Plaza del Marqués de Comillas plunges the visitor right into the Middle Ages. Not far from here stands the house in which St Isidore, patron-saint of Madrid, served as a valet. On 15 May the feast of St Isidore is celebrated with a dazzling *verbena*. The *verbena* is an open-air festival at which Madrid excels and which explodes with joy on summer nights, with fireworks, bells in full peal and prayers, after which the crowds go down to saunter along the banks of the Manzanares.

As you stroll among the old houses, surrounded by history, you find yourself immersed in the décor of another age, in the labyrinth of *callejones*, cross-roads and lanes that lead into the heart of this old quarter, the **Plaza Mayor**, a square expanse of sky and paving-stones flooded in light and enclosed by tall arcaded buildings. The arcades offer the visitor a refuge: here, on a café pavement, you can quench your thirst with a lemon *granizado* (water-ice). The spaciousness of the square matches the grandeur of its memories, for it was here, in this vast civil 'cloister' with its nine entrances, that the most dramatic ceremonies of bygone days were enacted. From the balcony of the Panadería the monarchs of Spain presided over bullfights, executions and *autos-da-fé*. A scene of excitement, violence and popular festivals, the

Madrid — the Rastro

The Rastro

Madrid — the Plaza Mayor

Plaza Mayor was also a place of culture, the theatre where the plays of Lope de Vega first triumphed. The equestrian statue of Philip III, the last witness of this turbulent past, stands in the centre of the square which he built for his own glory. The Plaza Mayor is less ambitious today and on Sundays a much more peaceful crowd gathers under its arcades – the philatelists of the famous stamp market.

As in all the cities of Europe, Sunday is also the day on which the flea market is held. Amid the bric-à-brac of the **Rastro**, in old Madrid, the visitor can rummage around and haggle in a market that fully justifies its reputation. Everything can be bought at the Rastro – furniture, pictures, sculptures and books in all styles, either genuine or copied, and even a bullfighter's costume. The crowd, just as bizarre as the market itself, provides a constant spectacle as the street-hawker offers a noisy mechanical figure for a few pesetas, while the *limpiabotas* has practically convinced you that your shoes need polishing and a small boy asks to be paid for the cigarette he has slipped into your hand. Amidst all the imploring voices a cry suddenly pierces the ear-drums: *'El gordo! Para hoy, para hoy! . . .'* ('The big prize! The draw is today! . . .'), as the blind vendor of lottery tickets offers you the chance of a fortune. *'Qué pregón!'* In Spain this is the cry of the hawkers; in a book about the Rastro, R. G. de la Serna says that 'to make a success of the *pregón*, the cry must be uttered in the form of a hook, a cry that twists and penetrates into the houses, into every nook and cranny, into the maze of passages . . .'. Amid the hullabaloo can be heard the quaint music of the *organillo*, a small organ from Barbary whose monotonous sounds are peculiar to Madrid. Alone in his shop, which is pervaded with the scents of rosewood and pine, the **stringed-instrument maker**, impervious to all this raucous bustle, quietly perfects the noble sounds of a guitar.

A stroll round the Rastro can be completed with an evening apéritif in one of the rustic bars in the lanes of old Madrid. A *manzanilla* with a few olives or other *tapas* sharpens the appetite for the specialities served in the local restaurants and taverns. The people of Madrid live by night, dining late and going to bed late. A last coffee can be taken on the Castellana and, if the dawn catches you unawares after a tour of the night-clubs, you can have a pre-breakfast snack of fritters and chocolate flavoured with cinnamon (*chocolate con churros*). In the streets you will see the last of the revellers in front of their doors, clapping their hands to call the *sereno*, the night-watchman who has the keys of the blocks of flats and comes to let them in.

Madrid – the bookstalls of the Rastro

The Rastro – shop of a stringed-instrument maker

3

FROM MADRID TO CÓRDOBA

Toledo – the Alcázar

At all hours of the day **Toledo** seems to throb, as if burning with an inner fire, but at dusk the dual miracle of nature and art is intensified as the setting sun bathes the 'imperial city' with its crimson and violet hues, shrouding it in flames and causing the waters of its river to sparkle.

Maurice Barrès, a fervent admirer of Toledo, describes the city with awe: 'Toledo remains a city built on a granite rock, harshly encircled by the deep ravine of the Tagus. In the middle of a motionless countryside, it forms an enormous cluster, a composite ascent of churches, monasteries, Gothic houses and high, narrow Arab passages.'

Crossing the Alcántara bridge, you come to the **Alcázar**, which had a turbulent history from the time of the Reconquest. From the top of the Alcázar you look down on to the 'imperial city', spread out before you like a map: here the cathedral, over there the terrace of San Juan de los Reyes with its statues, the Tagus flowing below the city and, near the Alcántara bridge, the ruins of the castle of San Servando; in the distance lies the plain of the Vega and on the other side of the river stand the *cigarrales*, country houses built in tiers with flowering gardens, where in the seventeenth century noble families liked to relax and monks held their retreats.

It would be difficult to find anywhere in the world such a mass of artistic riches concentrated in so small a space. In Toledo civilizations converged, interacting one with the other, and their passing has left a profusion of buildings that remain almost intact. But is not this city of ancient architecture also a dead city? Does not the similarity between the view of Toledo from the Alcántara bridge and that painted by El Greco in the sixteenth century prove that the city has presented the same profile for the past 400 years?

Under a stunning stormy sky, El Greco captured the quintessence of the city: this painting is a portrait rather than a landscape, a portrait of the same Toledo which the visitor sees today. Obviously, its situation has made Toledo

Toledo – view of the city

the prisoner of its river, so that the city has withdrawn into itself. Just as the Tagus has flowed imperturbably over the centuries along the bottom of the ravine, time has passed over Toledo without effecting any appreciable transformation since the moment when the last stone of its last building was laid. The transformations to be observed in Toledo do not belong to history, but are of a different order: a violet shadow, varying imperceptibly in size, a reflection of a beautiful Gothic façade, invisible a moment ago, a face that gazes at you with its large black eyes and leaves you with the fleeting impression that this grave stare comes from another age.

From the top of the Alcázar the visitor has already seen the single tower of the **cathedral** dominating the city like a lighthouse. Standing immediately below the cathedral, one is overpowered by this robust edifice and its compact forms, the product of a conquering faith. The construction of this most Spanish of cathedrals continued from the end of the thirteenth century until the end of the fifteenth, from the period when the Catholic religion lived in harmony

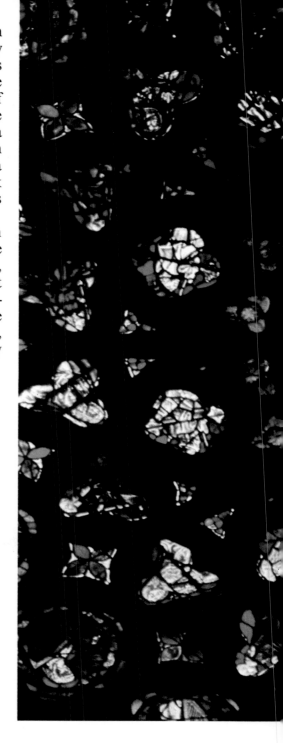

with the Muslim and Jewish religions until the time when it asserted its hegemony. The purest Gothic art is here seen to have absorbed Arab influences, especially in the interior decoration which is largely Mudejar. Inside the cathedral the visitor will find sculptures, grilles, altar-pieces and other marvels displayed in arrogant splendour.

Toledo — the cathedral

A rose-window of the cathedral

Blasco Ibáñez writes of a young Jewish beauty, 'with white complexion, almond eyes and heavy tresses of ebony', who listens to her nurse reciting old *romances* like this one:

> *In the city of Toledo,*
> *In the city of Granada,*
> *Is a dashing young man*
> *Named Diego León.*
> *He fell in love with Tamar,*
> *Who was a Jewess of Castile. . . .*

The harmony that existed between Muslims, Jews and Christians in medieval Spain resulted in frequent mixed marriages and countless touching love-stories in which the heroes were valorous Christian knights and the heroines beautiful Jewesses or languishing Moorish girls. But the hero could also be an Arab or a Jew and the lady of his dreams a Christian. This was the romantic aspect of the political concord which characterized the long periods of truce during the Reconquest.

Toledo, an Arab, Jewish and Christian city in the Middle Ages, has preserved many relics of this epoch. A visit to the two synagogues in the old Jewish quarter, in the south-west of the city, is strongly recommended. **Santa María la Blanca**, the older of the two, dates from the late twelfth century; it was converted into a church at the beginning of the fifteenth century, hence its name. Santa María la Blanca has a captivating stillness, a harmony of line and light. The horseshoe arches, the capitals and the glazed tiles (*azulejos*) are of the purest Moorish style. The other synagogue, El Tránsito, invites meditation and spiritual elevation. Its four walls are almost completely bare; the only decoration consists of a band of stucco along the upper part of the walls and some little ornamental arches.

Toledo – the synagogue of
Santa María la Blanca

The synagogue of Santa María la Blanca. Detail of the ceiling

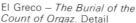

Toledo – the Casa del Greco

El Greco – *The Burial of the Count of Orgaz*

It is highly unlikely that El Greco ever lived in the house now known as the **Casa del Greco**. But this gentle distortion of historical truth should not deter the visitor from savouring this faithful reproduction of a sixteenth-century Toledan interior. In addition to its authentic furniture, it contains some important paintings by the artist, including the famous *View of Toledo*. From the patio you can admire the elegant rustic architecture of the house.

Born in Crete, El Greco (the name that he received during his stay in Venice) settled in Toledo around 1575 and remained there until his death in 1614. He identified himself with the city, making it his own, and by a strange process of mimesis the city began to resemble his paintings. This rebel, who in the heyday of the Renaissance painted Byzantine ascetics – emaciated faces, elongated bodies with limbs that seem to be detached like flames – this strange genius who wilfully disregarded the laws of anatomy, found in Toledo his spiritual home.

Not far from the Casa del Greco, in a chapel in the old church of Santo Tomé, is the dazzling **Burial of the Count of Orgaz**. The visitor should heed the injunction engraved in the slab above the painting: 'Even if you are in a hurry, O traveller, pause awhile and listen to an old story of our city. . . .' The inscription tells how Don Gonzalo Ruiz de Toledo, Count of Orgaz, was granted the remarkable honour, merited by his great piety, of being buried by the hands of St Augustine and St Stephen who descended from Heaven, in the year of grace 1312. The nobles present at the burial seem not to notice 'the miracle which is taking place before their eyes [and which] edifies them without astounding them'. Maurice Barrès continues: 'Why should they be surprised at being visited by these two saints, since they know that at this same moment the soul of the Count of Orgaz is appearing before the celestial court?'

Following pages: La Mancha

El Toboso – a woman whitewashing her house

El Toboso – a peasant

One cannot help recalling the 'Ingenious Hidalgo Don Quixote of La Mancha' when one approaches the great expanses of **La Mancha**, uninhabited for miles at a stretch, a horizon which the eyes scan wearily with nothing to attract their attention except, here and there, the famous windmills – a plain where the very skeleton of our planet is laid bare and which Cervantes immortalized, perhaps in derision, perhaps with affection. Pérez Galdós, the great Spanish novelist of the nineteenth century, was struck by the affinity that seems to exist between a real landscape and a character of fiction: 'Don Quixote needed this horizon . . . these lands furrowed by the path of hazard and adventure and where every happening seems due to chance or to the genies of fable; he needed this sun which melts the brains and makes wise men fools. . . .' Dulcinea del **Toboso**, transfigured by Don Quixote's amorous imagination, seems to be reborn in this photograph of a **woman** whitewashing her house. This laughing **peasant** could almost be Sancho Panza's brother or neighbour. The windmill in the photograph opposite is evocative of those immense stretches of solitude where windmills are the only signs of human industry: it is easy to see how a feverish imagination could turn them into malevolent beings, like the giants encountered by Don Quixote in 'The dreadful and unimaginable adventure of the windmills'.

'"What giants?" asked Sancho Panza.

'"Those you see there," replied his master, "with their long arms. Some giants have them about six miles long."

'"Take care, your worship," said Sancho; "those things over there are not giants but windmills, and what seem to be their arms are the sails, which are whirled round in the wind and make the millstone turn."

'"It is quite clear," replied Don Quixote, "that you are not experienced in this matter of adventures. They are giants, and if you are afraid, go away and say your prayers, whilst I advance and engage them in fierce and unequal battle."'

Don Quixote then advances to attack.

'At that moment a slight wind arose, and the great sails began to move. At the sight of which Don Quixote shouted: "Though you wield more arms than the giant Briareus, you shall pay for it!" Saying this, he commended himself with all his soul to his Lady Dulcinea, beseeching her aid in his great peril. Then, covering himself with his shield and putting his lance in the rest, he urged Rosinante forward at a full gallop and attacked the nearest windmill, thrusting his lance into the sail. But the wind turned it with such violence that it shivered his weapon in pieces, dragging the horse and his rider with it, and sent the knight rolling badly injured across the plain.' (From Cervantes: *Don Quixote* translated by J. M. Cohen, Penguin Classics, 1950. Reprinted by permission of Penguin Books Ltd.)

La Mancha – a village

4
CÓRDOBA

Córdoba
Remote and lonely.
Black mare, huge moon,
And olives in my saddle-bag.
Although I know the roads,
I'll never reach Córdoba.

Federico García Lorca.

Córdoba – the Patio de los Naranjos

Córdoba is like a fallen city abandoned on the shores of time. It seems remote and inaccessible, left by men to grow old in loneliness, counting past glories. Time and time again this city, once known as the 'Sultana', managed to rise from its ashes, but today, exhausted by all its metamorphoses, it languishes in the heart of Andalusia. Yet Córdoba can still take pride in its supreme glory, the mosque, which one reaches by passing through the **Patio de los Naranjos** and the scent of its orange-trees.

Under the Roman Empire this city was the capital of Hispania Ulterior and from this period of its first splendour it has preseved a majestic **Roman bridge**. Between the eighth and eleventh centuries it was transformed into the capital of Muslim Spain; the seat of the court of the caliphs of the West, it was 'the ornament of the world', the most brilliant intellectual centre in Europe. With its philosophers, the Jew Maimonides and the Muslim Averroës, the city of the upper Guadalquivir carried on the torch of civilization and gave Europe, then plunged in barbarism, access to the heritage of Antiquity.

Córdoba – Roman bridge

The 'forest of Córdoba', as the mosque is sometimes known, presents a fantastic combination of interweaving forms and straight lines, subtlety and balance, profusion and austerity, in a kind of labyrinth where the visitor senses that, beyond his immediate aesthetic emotion, he will attain a wisdom which he cannot yet define but for which he yearns.

When Abd-er-Rahman I decided on the construction of the original **mosque** in 785, he wanted a building as sumptuous as the temples of the East. During subsequent reigns and up to the tenth century, the mosque was frequently altered and enlarged, the aisles and columns steadily increasing in number. To support this colossal mass, horseshoe arches were erected one above the other, with alternating voussoirs of stone and brick. This ingenious solution gives the mosque an airy and wonderfully balanced appearance. Under El Akham II the decoration, hitherto fairly austere, became more extravagant. The foiled arch was introduced, as can be seen on the **east front**. A few centuries later, the mosque became a cathedral and the chased silver **Paschal Lamb** in the chancel symbolizes the entry of Christianity into the Muslim temple.

Although it has suffered the ravages of time, the mosque's crenellated

Córdoba – decorated arches in the mosque

The mosque — a general view of the interior

The mosque — foiled arch of the east front

The mosque — Paschal Lamb in the chancel

Córdoba — the mosque,
dome of the Kebla

enclosure-wall has retained its power and some of its gateways have preserved their resplendent beauty intact. Going through the Puerta del Perdón, you come into the **Patio de los Naranjos** (Court of Oranges), 'a garden of water and sun, stone and shadow'. The aisles of Abd-er-Rahman I extend before you in a diminishing perspective that vanishes into a rosy half-light. The columns multiply endlessly and the impression of similarity given by an overall view is misleading, for no column is identical to its neighbour. There are more than a thousand, of granite, jasper and precious marbles not only from Spain, but also from France, Constantinople and Carthage. As if this were not enough, even the capitals have a history of their own; some are Visigothic, others Roman or Arabic.

Meanwhile the eye, momentarily fascinated by all this detail, tries to master the vast and complex geometry. Alas, one's visual enchantment is brutally shattered. After the Reconquest the Catholic Church would not tolerate the existence of the mosque which, in its harmony, proclaimed the superiority of the vanquished. That superiority had to be crushed and so the aisles, which had previously opened on to the patio, were closed and the edifice surrounded with chapels. In 1523 the chapter of canons, intent on completing the alterations, decided to build a Christian cathedral inside the mosque, part of which had to be demolished. When Charles V discovered the disaster it was too late and the emperor exclaimed: 'What you are doing can be found anywhere, what you once had exists nowhere else.'

But one must try to forget this offence against beauty. As you continue your tour of the mosque, you will come to some 'chapels' such as the Capilla de Villaviciosa or the Capilla Real, where the exuberant stucco decoration contrasts with the austerity of the original mosque. The foiled arches intersect one another and a network of ribbing divides and supports the dome. Nothing, however, equals the splendour of the mihrab and its vestibule, the **Kebla**, the **dome** of which is a pure marvel. The presence of the Koran in the mihrab niche gave the latter its sacred

Córdoba – the Patio de los Naranjos

aura; this sanctuary within a sanctuary is entirely covered with arabesques and mosaics which display the supreme refinement attained by Muslim art in the tenth century. The faithful said their prayers in front of the niche, which faces in the direction of Mecca.

After the Reconquest, Córdoba was relegated to the position of a mistress who suddenly finds herself in disgrace. The Christians allowed industry to dwindle and the admirable irrigation works constructed by the Arabs to fall into decay. But the old master craftsmen have left their permanent mark on the city and its inhabitants.

The picturesque old quarters of

Córdoba lie round the mosque-cathedral, between the Guadalquivir and Avenida Gran Capitán. The names of some of the districts and streets commemorate the traditional craftsmen of Córdoba – the parchment-makers, the soap-makers, the saddlers and the perfumers. Even today the **craftsmen's shops** are still numerous; here, in the atmosphere of an Oriental *souk*, the visitor is offered all the typical products of Córdoba: gold and silver-ware, tanned and painted leather, or embossed leather decorated with gold.

Théophile Gautier has this to say about Córdoba, the 'Sultana' reduced to slavery: 'Córdoba has a more

Córdoba – craftsmen's shops

African appearance than any other city in Andalusia; its streets, or rather its lanes, with their chaotic paving-stones resembling the bed of a dry torrent, have nothing about them to remind one of the customs or habits of Europe. One walks along interminable chalk-coloured walls, the occasional window latticed with grilles and bars, and the only persons one meets are a beggar with an unprepossessing face, a pious woman in a black hood, or a *majo* flying past like lightning on his brown horse. . . . If the Moors could return, they would not have to do much to re-establish themselves there.' Things have certainly changed a little since Gautier's time, but one has only to stroll along the lanes of the **Judería**, the old Jewish quarter, to discover their narrowness and the same refreshing coolness and stillness which the Frenchman must have known in the nineteenth century.

A few more twists and turns through these endless lanes and you come into Calle Maimónides, opposite the synagogue, a modest but charming building which dates from the fourteenth century and is the only remaining synagogue in Andalusia; inside, the visitor will find some excellent decoration of stucco-work intermingled with Hebrew inscriptions. The house of the Jewish philosopher Maimonides stands on the square which bears his name. This old building houses the municipal museum, which contains an impressive collection of pictures on the art of bullfighting and mementoes of a popular local hero, the *torero* Manolete.

Suddenly, the chords of a guitar break the silence:

And then begin the tears
of the guitar. . . .

Lorca.

This melody and others pursue you as you stroll at random through the

Córdoba – craftsman's shop in the Judería

squares and **lanes**, the *callejones* and *callejuelas* with their evocative names: Callejón de las Flores, de los Rincones de Oro, de los Siete Infantes de Lara. . . . Now and again, as you pass along the beautiful white walls, the inquisitive eye catches a glimpse of the famous patios of Córdoba; whether of lordly splendour or of more modest proportions, they all have in their centre a fountain from which a jet of water spurts, with a mass of plants and flowers all around and *azulejos* (glazed tiles) on the walls. A rocking-chair sways to and fro, revealing that it was occupied only a moment ago. At the threshold a breath of cool air envelops and draws the visitor, but discretion forbids one to cross this threshold, to violate its privacy. As one strolls on, this contact with an art of living inherited from the Arabs causes the mind to wander in search of the past. How did people live in these houses, which for Arab women were both palaces and prisons? The poets have written of the beautiful slave-girls and favourites who kindled passions and fanned the flames of hatred. They have also sung of the beautiful Moorish girls who did not hesitate to break the Muslim law by taking a lover. One girl, Marién, spent her childhood in a harem under the eye of her mother. Her father married her off without her ever having met the man who was to be her husband. It was then that her life as a recluse really began. She had to share with other women the husband whom she had not herself chosen. Her whole life was spent thus: the prisoner of these walls, she was both queen and servant. As a young woman she served only her husband, whom she had to conquer anew each day; when she grew old she was discarded and had no choice but to serve the entire household. Never once did her kingdom pass beyond these frontiers.

Córdoba – the Plaza del Potro

Córdoba – a lane in the Judería

Just as the cathedral was planted forcibly in the very heart of the mosque, the white walls of the houses have been covered with **holy images** and the squares with scenes of the Crucifixion proclaiming the triumph of Catholicism. These manifestations of popular piety show a certain ostentation. Some are touching in their naïveté, while others are imbued with an elegant beauty, like the famous Cristo de los Faroles in which the figure of Christ is surrounded by four lamps. There are also a great many monasteries and churches built in a mixture of styles – Romanesque, Gothic and Mudejar – with square towers that were originally minarets. When one sees Córdoba draped in its whiteness and observes its essentially Oriental aspect, one wonders which has really triumphed – the Cross or the Crescent?

It has to be with regret that one leaves this captivating city, inscrutable and luminous like a poem by Góngora, the most celebrated of Córdoba's sons.

Córdoba – the roofs seen from the cathedral

Córdoba – Holy images

Instead of following the valley of the Guadalquivir, the road from Córdoba to Seville cuts across the *campiñas* and at Ecija meets the Genil, a tributary of the great Andalusian river. The Genil flows along the bottom of its narrow valley, turning the wheels of the oil and flour mills among the *huertas* (areas of irrigated, cultivated land). At Ecija the traveller is already in the Sevillian countryside; the town has benefited from the prosperity of its great neighbour, acquiring churches and Renaissance or Baroque palaces such as the **Benamejí Palace** with its elaborately decorated façade. The way of life here is a foretaste of Seville; the men, women and children have the lively grace of the Andalusian people of the plain. In the cafés of the Plaza Mayor the men talk excitedly in singing accents, their words flying to and fro and their eyes sparkling mischievously. The women fan themselves nonchalantly.

The road continues through the sun-drenched *campiñas*. The crops of cereals make way for olive-trees which extend in rigidly straight lines as far as the eye can see:

> *Old olive-trees thirsty*
> *Under the bright sun of the day,*
> *The dusty olive-groves*
> *Of the fields of Andalusia!*
>
> Machado.

Soon you come to Carmona, at the top of a hill overlooking a fertile plain (*vega*). The Romans made this a strategic position and Carmona, perched on its rock, is enclosed by solid Roman walls that were modified by the Arabs. The walls are pierced with powerful gateways, the Puerta de Córdoba and the **Puerta de Sevilla**. Never has Seville seemed so far away!

Carmona — Puerta de Sevilla

Ecija — Benamejí palace

5
SEVILLE

Seville — the Tower of Gold

Quién no ha visto Sevilla
No ha visto maravilla!

'He who has not seen Seville has not seen a marvel!' In contrast with the contemplative atmosphere of Córdoba, **Seville** offers herself to the visitor with all the impudence of a beautiful Andalusian. The allure of Seville lies in its grace, its nonchalance, its *douceur de vivre*, the strange light in which everything vibrates in the *calina*, a haze of heat that blurs distances. It is an intense heat, sometimes exasperating, but allayed by the cool splashing of a fountain and perfumed with strong whiffs of jasmin and orange-blossom from the surrounding gardens. In such an atmosphere one is hardly surprised that Don Juan should have been a Sevillian and, as one muses by the fountain of the **Plaza de los Reyes**, one understands why 'the legend of Don Juan has gone round the world, imbued with all the fragrance and extravagance of a Seville carnival, like the old Levantine ships that returned from Ceylon laden with spices'. (Ortega y Gasset)

Seville lies huddled in a majestic curve of the Guadalquivir. For centuries ships have sailed up to this port firmly ensconced in the plain; in the sixteenth century the gold of the Indies was taken from stranded ships and immediately converted into doubloons at the Casa de la Moneda. At this time the city seethed with activity: the gateway to the Americas, it was the meeting-place of travellers, rich merchants and bankers, adventurers, vagabonds and *pícaros*, a whole world with which Cervantes was familiar and which he depicted in his *Novelas Ejemplares*.

On the left bank of the river stands the **Torre del Oro** (Tower of Gold); the pride of the Moors and then of reconquered Spain, the tower seems still to be waiting for some mysterious cargo of treasure.

Seville — the Plaza de los Reyes

Seville — Holy Week, the *paso* of the Virgen del Valle

Seville — the Giralda

Seville — the cathedral

Seville — Holy Week, hooded penitent

The **Giralda**, the tower of the **cathedral** and once a minaret, watches jealously over Seville. But the city has other protectors:

> *Virgin in a crinoline,*
> *Virgin of solitude,*
> *Open like a huge tulip*
> *On your vessel of light,*
> *You furrow*
> *The high tide*
> *Of the city. . . .*

In this poem entitled *Saeta*, Lorca sings of the queens of the popular quarters of Seville, the miraculous Virgin of Hope, the 'Macarena', and the **Virgin del Valle** (Virgin of the Valley), who are almost indistinguishable one from the other. In Holy Week they leave their modest churches, dressed like dolls in brocade and velvet, decked out in the gold and jewels of the faithful, who cheer them wildly. These statues, representing all the hopes of the people, are the symbols of a naïve and touching piety, almost primitive in its fervour, under the inscrutable gaze of the **hooded penitents.**

Seville — the Plaza de España
Holy Week procession

Holy Week in Seville is an awe-inspiring and disturbing glimpse of medieval Spain reborn. Religion is present everywhere, austere and hysterical. For seven days the bruised body of Christ and statues of Our Lady of Sorrows, surrounded by military uniforms, are carried in an interminable procession. The brilliantly coloured altars (*pasos*), swamped in flowers, wobble along the streets. The **encapuchados**, members of the local religious brotherhoods, walk in front of the processions, 'strange unicorns' in hoods pierced with two gleaming black holes who at night, amid muffled drum-rolls and clanking chains, seem to be leading the people to an *auto-da-fé*. Suddenly the procession halts. A man comes forward, his eyes wild with ecstasy, and his cry shatters the silence. To the passing statue of the Virgin or of Christ he offers a *saeta*, a song of love and compassion improvised in an uncontrolled frenzy of mystical ardour. The *saeta* is sung only during Holy Week, otherwise it brings bad luck, say superstitious believers. . . .

But Holy Week in Seville is not only meditation and piety. By contrast with the tragic ceremonies of Castile, the Andalusians prefer the external manifestations of Catholicism and the popularity of the spectacular **processions** draws tourists from all over the world. Among the flocks of penitents and the crowds eager for public merry-making, the religious and the pagan mingle freely. For these seven days the atmosphere of Seville is festive rather than devotional.

During this time the deserted **Plaza de España** offers a haven to those in need of solitude.

Seville — the *encapuchados*

Seville – the Romería del Rocío

Horsewomen

There is nothing quite like the colourful atmosphere of Andalusian festivals, even the religious festivals. Easter and Corpus Christi are important *romerías*, but the most typical is Pentecost, the **Romería del Rocío**. From Seville to Almonte, the gipsies in their waggons drawn by oxen – a mass of multicoloured flowers, cretonnes and flounces – the Figaros parading on horseback with their Carmens riding behind them, and the alluring **horsewomen** dressed in black, together form a joyful procession to escort the 'Sin Pecado' (the 'Sinless'), a statue of the Virgin in a travelling shrine drawn by two young oxen.

All this Andalusian jollity inevitably reaches its climax with wine and guitars, dancing and bullfights (*corridas*). In the afternoon, as they wait for five o'clock, the *aficionados* and tourists gather in the glorious coolness of the **María Luisa park** or the Murillo gardens, impatient to acclaim the great heroes of the bull-ring. Foreign visitors always make a visit to the Barrio de Santa Cruz, the most picturesque district of the city, which presents the kind of Andalusian décor that one might expect to find in an operetta. Among the lanes with their flowering balconies and wrought-iron work is hidden the enchanting **Patio of the Museum of the Brotherhoods**, which the visitor will probably find only after some difficulty, having gone back on his tracks at least a dozen times in this magical labyrinth.

Seville – Patio of the Museum of the Brotherhoods

Seville – the María Luisa park

Seville — suburb of Triana

In summer Seville declares open war on the sun. In the photograph opposite the old Andalusian of **Triana** can meditate in the cool shade provided by the roof of cane. In the full heat of the summer the **Calle de las Sierpes** (Street of Serpents), if photographed from the same angle, would have been almost completely hidden by the *toldos* or sun-blinds which jut out in front of nearly every house.

There are no cars in the Calle de las Sierpes. The street belongs to pedestrians. It is the meeting-place for the inhabitants of Seville and has a village atmosphere in which everybody seems to know everybody else, recognizing and greeting one another with a peculiarly Andalusian exuberance. They talk business, have a drink, linger in the shops and stroll endlessly up and down the street. As in Madrid, there are *casinos*, those vast café-clubs, long and dark, where 'fashionable' gentlemen, sunk in their leather armchairs, chat, play cards and wait for time to pass. In the bullfighting season the *aficionados* make voluble comments and forecasts about the future masters of the ring.

Seville — Calle de las Sierpes

El Cordobés

Seville — the Plaza de Toros

Aparicio

A bull about to enter the ring

Dominguín

What has drawn the attention of **El Cordobés** and **Luis Miguel Dominguín**, dressed in their dazzling costumes? The bull they are about to confront, or the bravery of **Aparicio** who kneels to tame his adversary? The bulls are allocated to the *toreros* by the drawing of lots (*sorteo*). The poster showing these three gods of the bull-ring may well be displayed at the **Plaza de Toros** during your stay in Seville.

El Cordobés

Antequera

The marsh of the Guadalquivir, near Seville

Little villages like **Antequera**, perched on high ground, with dazzling walls, streets of beaten earth or paved with slippery pebbles, and a chequerwork pattern of old tiled roofs, are scattered all over the Sevillian countryside, a region scorched by a pitiless sun but mercifully refreshed by the waters of the Guadalquivir and numerous other rivers. The **lakes** in the environs of **Bornos** form natural reservoirs. The

Lake near Bornos

soil is rich and ideal for cultivation, but Andalusia, a land of large estates – the latifundia – has long remained devoted to stockraising and hunting, resisting all development. However, projects for irrigation, draining the brackish marshes, and repopulation are now restoring to the province a little of its former prosperity. In ancient times the land of Baetica enjoyed a reputation for great fertility and the Romans came here to gather the cereals, wine and oil which they needed.

The delta of the Guadalquivir is occupied by the **Marismas**, a region of swamps and lagoons that have slowly been filled with alluvia. The river is the great lord, promising miraculous riches and wonderful opportunities for fishing, but wild and dangerous when in spate.

As in the Camargue in southern France, **horses** and **cattle** have been reared here since the Middle Ages. The *vaqueros*, in sombreros and leather trousers, tend the herds, counting the animals, branding them and leading them to the fresh-water pools scattered over the vast marshland. The rearing of bulls for the arena is a traditional activity and some *ganaderías* in Andalusia are famous well beyond the frontiers of Spain.

The *cortijos* or Andalusian farms, the symbol of the great landowner, are barely visible, lost amid the fields. Sometimes, in the full heat of the day, one meets a man on horseback who, under his broad-rimmed hat, watches over his master's lands. Here, the present has not yet freed itself from a feudal past.

But Andalusia is also the country of the sierras, green at the bottom and bare at the top. A dry cold and the sun beating down! The village of **Montefrío**, by its very name and the brightness of its light, evokes the stark extremes of this temperamental climate.

Andalusian horses

Andalusian bulls

Montefrío

6

GRANADA

The Alhambra, Hall of the Abencerrages. Detail

A rare pleasure awaits the traveller who visits **Granada**; like the open pomegranate which is the symbol of the city (*granada* means 'pomegranate'), it unfolds at the foot of the **Sierra Nevada**, the jagged peaks glittering in the sun. Between the hill on which the **Alhambra** fortress stands and the hill over which the suburb of Albaicín lies, the Darro flows along the bottom of a ravine. Granada enjoys a marvellous situation and climate. Yet to love this city is a secret which the traveller must learn for himself. 'The carefree traveller, full of smiles and the noise of locomotives, goes to the *Fallas* of Valencia. . . . The melancholy, contemplative traveller goes to Granada, to be alone amid the scent of orange-blossom and moss and the trills of the nightingale which rise from the old hills, near the walls of the Alhambra, a pyre of saffron, dark grey and blotting-paper pink. To be alone.' The name of Federico García Lorca, the author of this tender evocation of Granada and its Alhambra, has become associated with that of the city with which he fell in love and whose praises he sang as no one else has done. It was in Granada – 'his Granada', says another poet, Antonio Machado – that Lorca was shot in 1936.

Wandering through the quiet streets of the Albaicín, one's thoughts turn to the poet who so perfectly expressed the lyrical and dramatic essence of this Moorish quarter: 'the timid, fantastic Albaicín, the city of barking dogs and plaintive guitars, of dark nights in the white-walled streets, the tragic Albaicín of superstition, of sorceresses who cast spells and summon the spirits of the dead, the city of strange gipsy rituals, cabalistic signs and amulets, of seductresses and bloody maledictions, passionate Albaicín. . . .'

A visit to the Alhambra, the city within the city, brings one surprise after another; its most astounding feature is the richness of the decoration, which can be seen in this photograph of a section of wall in the **Sala de los**

The Alhambra and the Sierra Nevada

Abencerrages (Hall of the Abencerrages).

Who could express the splendour of the **Alhambra** better than the Arabs themselves? Ibn Zamrak, one of the greatest poets of Muslim Spain, glorifies the beauty of the Sabika, the hill on which the Alhambra stands, in these words:

'Pause on the Esplanade of the Sabika and look around you: the city is a lady who is being joined in wedlock with the hillside. . . .

'The Sabika is a crown placed on the forehead of Granada, a crown in which the stars themselves would willingly become encrusted.

'And the Alhambra – God protect it – is the ruby surmounting this crown.'

At first sight the Alhambra is merely a fortress with solid walls. But the walls and square towers are there only to protect from the outside world the miracle of fragile delicacy that one discovers on passing through one of the gateways. In the thirteenth century the founder of the Nasrid dynasty established his residence in the Alcázar, which has since vanished, and it was not until the fourteenth century that his descendants had the present palace built. The Alhambra was conceived for a life of luxury, love and merry-making. The tough Maugrabin warriors of the early years of Arab domination had become softened by court life and its intrigues. The edifice is both a striking testimony to this decadence and a unique artistic marvel.

The capture of Granada, the last Muslim bastion, by the Catholic Kings in 1492 marked the end of the Reconquest and also the end of Muslim civilization in Spain. Boabdil, the weak 'little king', had to flee from the city. Pausing on the hill to have a last look at his kingdom and the palace in which he had lived, Boabdil sighed; the place where he stopped still bears the name 'Suspiro del Moro' ('Sigh of the Moor').

One of the charms of the palace is that it seems to have been built without any apparent plan; according to the whims of successive sovereigns, it was constantly enlarged until it became a jumble of patios, pools, intimate alcoves and huge rooms. Each part of the enormous building is a masterpiece of proportion, both in architecture and in decoration. The **Patio de los Leones** (Court of the Lions) is undoubtedly the most famous place in the Alhambra. In the centre of the court stands the fountain with twelve crudely carved lions; perfect in its harmony, the court is surrounded by arcades supported by white marble columns. From this patio one enters the **Sala de los Reyes** (Hall of the Kings), decorated with stalactite arches and domed vaulting (*media naranja*). At the end of this room are the palace's only **paintings**, no doubt representing Moorish kings of Granada.

The Alhambra – the ceiling of the Hall of the Kings

The Alhambra – the Patio de los Leones

On one side of the **Patio de los Leones** is the Sala de las Dos Hermanas (Hall of the Two Sisters), decorated with gorgeous stucco-work and faience tiling. In the Hall of the Abencerrages, opposite, legend has it that thirty-six Muslim knights were murdered by order of King Boabdil. The most accomplished example of Nasrid ornamentation is the Hall of the Ambassadors, with its inscriptions, its geometric interlacings and the wild exuberance of its stucco vegetation. In front of this hall lies the serenely delicate Patio de los Arrayanes (Court of the Myrtles).

Granada is bathed in the perfume of flowers, particularly jasmin, and hums with the sound of water splashing in the fountains and ornamental lakes. These scents and murmurs seem to be redoubled at the **Generalife**, the magnificent summer residence of the Nasrid sovereigns, overlooking the Alhambra, the city and its fertile *vega*. Here, the description of paradise in the Koran seems to have been realized: 'a luxuriant garden, of a deep green verging on black and furrowed by delicious streams'.

Granada – the Generalife

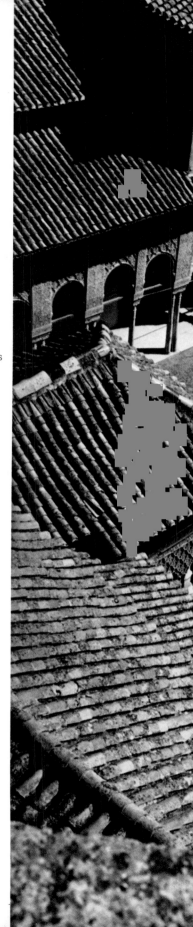

The Alhambra – the Patio de los Leones

Granada — courtyard of a house

Granada — the market in the Plaza Larga

Granada — the sacristy of the Carthusian monastery

Inside the walls of the **Sacromonte** the **gipsies** have entrenched themselves in a permanent camp. In the caves (*cuevas*) of the rock, where the gipsy families have settled, they have created all the atmosphere of a home: the gleaming white walls are gaily decorated with copper utensils, pottery, trinkets and framed photographs. The life of the gipsies is divided between music, dancing and commerce, for they sell their tribal folklore to tourists: in the evening the Sacromonte is illuminated as men and women, posted in front of each doorway and contemptuously soliciting the custom of visitors, each claim to offer the best entertainment. Castanets and guitars set the rhythm for the pleasant, broken cadence of the *zambra* or for the gaiety of a *rumba gitana*. Hands are clapped, songs are

Gipsy festival at the Sacromonte

sung and heels are stamped; the women, in their tight-fitting *traje de lunares*, flaunt their haughty elegance.

A word of warning to tourists: the gipsies are simply doing you a favour, but if, by chance, they are carried away by the intoxication of the dance, the performance then becomes a genuine primitive ritual – their bodies are contorted in excitement, their eyes flash, they utter cries as if in a trance, and the rhythm grows more frantic, as the magic spell of music and song takes them back to the very origins of their race. You are strangers, longing to unveil a secret, to penetrate a mystery which you can never share! You must therefore be content to be discreet spectators of a ceremony in which the gipsy loses himself totally in a world inaccessible to outsiders.

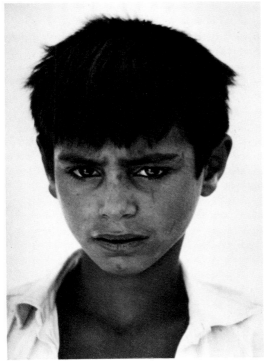

A young gipsy

A goat of the Alpujarra

Granada – Sacromonte

103

A gipsy girl

A gipsy in *traje de lunares*

Granada — Sacromonte

Sacromonte

The village of Capileira in the Alpujarra, to the south of Granada

A herd of sheep in the Alpujarra

It might almost seem as if the mountain scene and the skier in the photographs had found their way into this book by mistake. Such scenery is certainly unusual in Andalusia. But, if the snow of the sierra provides an unexpected contrast to the green *vega* of Granada and an even more startling contrast to the barren lands of the **Alpujarra** (*preceding page*), it is no mirage. As early as October the peaks of the **Sierra Nevada** are covered with snow and the people of Granada can indulge in the joys of skiing right up to May.

Those who enjoy an abrupt change of landscape can take the Veleta road, the highest in Europe, which leads from the Arab palaces of Granada to the snows of the mountains. From the top of the **Picacho de Veleta** one looks out over the abyss of the Corral; on each side of this chasm the gigantic rock-faces of the Veleta, the Pico Mulhacén (3,481 metres, the highest peak in Spain) and the Alcazaba confront each other. At the bottom of the terrifying ravines thunder the torrents which eventually combine to form the Genil. To the south, in the distance, one can see the gleaming silver-blue sea and, even further away, shimmering in an unreal light, the mountains of the Rif in Morocco.

The Picacho de Veleta, in the Sierra Nevada

7

FROM GRANADA TO BARCELONA

Guadix – interior of troglodyte dwelling

On leaving Granada the traveller finds himself in a sun-scorched landscape reminiscent of the African steppes, without the slightest trace of vegetation; here and there a man or woman can be seen, dressed in black and riding an unwilling donkey. The rivers in this region evaporate or are absorbed by the thirsty earth. And yet suddenly, amid all this desolation, appears the Oriental town of **Guadix**.

As soon as the car stops you will be assailed by a swarm of brown children with black eyes glittering like pieces of coal and their hair across their foreheads, engagingly aggressive. Each of them will offer to show you round the town for a few pesetas. The most determined child, or perhaps the one with the most amusing appearance, will win and the rest will scamper off to find other visitors. Their persistence is partly a game, certainly, but also partly an attempt to compensate for their pitiable fate. The visitor should therefore not be too irritated by their entreaties, even if they are sometimes a nuisance; these mercurial urchins, dirty and ragged, are much too proud to accept pity or charity and it is a service that they are offering in the hope of alleviating their poverty. One of them will take you to the **troglodyte dwellings** of Guadix – the Barrio de Santiago – and the surrounding area. These houses are hollowed out of the tufa and inhabited mainly by gipsies. With their roofs level with the ground and their projecting chimneys, they could almost be the creation of some *avant-garde* town-planner. The façades, retaining-walls and chimneys reflect a dazzling light: every year the exteriors of the *cuevas* are given a new coat of whitewash, as are the **interiors**, which are simple like their inhabitants.

Guadix – troglodyte dwellings

Vélez Blanco — the village below the castle

Vélez Blanco — the castle

Not many maps mention **Vélez Blanco**. Why, then, should such a modest village attract our attention? Vélez Blanco has a special surprise in store for the visitor, for at the beginning of the sixteenth century the delicate art of the Italian Renaissance found its way into this remote Andalusian village. The powerful Marquises de Los Vélez commissioned Italian architects and artists to build and decorate a splendid **castle** at the top of a hill overlooking the village and its flat-roofed houses. From the top of the hill there is a magnificent view of the bare mountains, sometimes tinged with pink and outlined against an implacably blue sky. The castle, polygonal in plan and flanked by crenellated towers, has a haughty elegance. But this beautiful exterior is a body without a soul. All that remains of the interior is a court, a marble staircase and some armorial bearings; the rest (in other words, practically everything) was bought and transported to New York in 1903. The visitor's disappointment is all the greater because the architecture of the exterior seemed so promising.

Near Vélez Blanco, at the extremity of the Sierra de María, amateur archaeologists can visit the **Cueva de los Letreros** (Cave of the Signs), which is decorated with prehistoric drawings and red paintings. A great many similar caves are to be found in the neighbourhood and there are even some rocks out in the open which bear signs carved by the hand of man in prehistoric times.

Vélez Blanco — the Cueva de los Letreros

Murcia offers a sudden vision of freshness, for here the muddy Segura washes the fertile lands of the *huerta*. All the wealth of produce grown in the region is displayed in the markets. The fruits present a variety of appetizing colours and thirst-quenching juices and you should sample some of the succulent little pears, the figs which taste like honey, or a bunch of fragrant grapes. You can then stroll along the busy streets which are shaded by sun-blinds (*toldos*), pausing at one of the numerous cafés which offer an incredible variety of snacks (*tapas*) – various kinds of pork, vegetables, fish and shell-fish, just enough for a tasty mouthful, with a glass of the sparkling local wine or an aniseed cordial.

The secret of the golden-pink colouring of Murcia is the adobe, a brick of mud and straw dried in the sun. This modest rustic material attains a genuine architectural dignity in the palaces and churches which you discover as you follow the twists and turns of the streets. The **cathedral** is particularly impressive and is undoubtedly the greatest Baroque edifice in Spain, with the intricate decoration of its Rococo façade and the tower from the top of which one can see the whole of the *huerta* of Murcia.

Murcia

Murcia – the cathedral

trees offer more than their fruit, for the palm-leaves also provide revenue. The palms are tied to the tree, which then loses its magnificent plumes and assumes the slightly grotesque appear-

Elche — the palm plantation

Suddenly one seems to be in Africa, the Africa of one's dreams. At **Elche**, in the most suffocating heat to be found anywhere in Spain, the traveller discovers an enchanting oasis where the eyes can rest after the constant dryness of Andalusia. The streets are narrow and the perfumes heady; the light, so garish in this region, is allowed to penetrate into the flat-topped houses only through narrow slits. The men and women, who are occupied in making *alpargatas* (hemp sandals), have dark brown skin and raven-black hair.

Eighty thousand palm-trees encircle the town, some solitary and aloof, the others standing more sociably in groups. In the canals their reflections are multiplied endlessly in an interplay of shapes, lines, shadow and light. The **palm plantation** is the pride of the town and its chief source of prosperity. The date harvest, the most important activity of the year, takes place in winter. But the

ance of an enormous paint-brush rising into the sky; the palms whiten in the shade and, as Holy Week approaches, are dispatched throughout Spain for the Palm Sunday processions and to decorate the balconies of towns and villages. The consecrated palm, it seems, possesses the power of averting lightning.

Alicante — Explanada de España

The countryside of Andalusia has now made way for the Mediterranean scenery of the Costa Blanca which, with its watercolour tints and subdued light, is among the most attractive in Spain. The beaches of golden sand stretch along an unruffled sea.

As you walk slowly along the **Explanada de España** its wavy coloured bands seem to rock in perpetual motion. You will probably be overcome by a deliciously lazy feeling and you may wonder if Alicante is perhaps the haven for which you have been longing. But, if you are drawn by the graceful forms of the **hills** outlined in the distance against the bright horizon, you will want to set off once more and discover the fragrant wild plants that grow among the slender almond-trees.

Further to the north, the massive shape of the **Peñon d'Ifach** rises from a suddenly turbulent sea. All that remains of this old volcano is an enormous pillar of lava which forms the peñon, moulded in the shape of the volcano's throat.

In the environs of Alicante
The Peñon d'Ifach

Guadalest

The main road from Alicante to Valencia runs along the coast. Since the sea is there, the east coast is naturally picturesque, like any seaboard region, a succession of smooth beaches interrupted by the cliffs of the Cabo de la Nao or by little islands such as Ifach and Benidorm. But, though pretty enough, this route gives the traveller little sense of being in a foreign land. The modern world has installed its wealthy bathing resorts, which have not managed to escape the stereotyped and pretentious vulgarity of town-planning. Tourists, attracted by the guarantee of sunshine, have erected long lines of modern blocks, a continuous wall of concrete which in many places has encroached on the surrounding countryside.

If you prefer to savour a prouder and more authentic Spain, leave the coast at Benidorm and take the inland road, which winds its way through bleak mountains. The sun beats down more fiercely here and the more austere Spain reappears.

This inland road will bring you to the little village of **Guadalest**, just like an eagle's nest, surrounded by precipitous slopes. A tunnel hewn out of the rock provides the only way into the village. Most of the inhabitants live inside the castle enclosure; the narrow, winding streets lead up to the cemetery, where there is a fine panorama of the castle and the mountain.

View of Guadalest from the castle

The Albufera

Orange-trees near Valencia

Blasco Ibáñez has written lovingly and at great length of the **Valencia region**, its beauty, its richness and its dramas. The **Albufera** provides the background for some of his novels; a fishermen's paradise and a refuge for migrating waterfowl, the lagoon is slowly silting up and in its alluvial marshland large rice-plantations have appeared to which Valencian gastro-

122

The Albufera

nomy owes its famous *paella*. Scattered over the fields are the last *barracas*, the modest dwellings of the small farmers, with whitewashed walls of dried mud and straw roofs.

The Albufera is also the 'little sea', as the Arabs called it. It should be seen at dawn, when the immense silvery-pink lake merges with the sky and the boat of an eel-fisherman can be seen hovering among the reeds. At this hour the strangely bare lagoon assumes the subdued hues of a Scandinavian lake, offering a moment of perfect stillness, of reverie and communion with nature.

Valencia – the Palacio del Marqués de Dos Aguas

Valencia, the city of El Cid, abounds in architectural riches – churches, towers, steeples, palaces and domes faced with mosaic. The **Palacio del Marqués de Dos Aguas** is a Rococo jewel with an elaborately ornate doorway conceived by the frenzied imagination of the painter Hipólito Rovina, who died insane. To each side of a wrought-iron gate, two atlantes straight from the world of Michelangelo seem to be supporting the whole edifice. Above these symmetrical figures a Virgin and Child, simple but almost incongruous, completes an unusual trio.

In Valencia every Thursday, in front of the cathedral, the **Water Court** holds its sessions under the Porch of the Apostles.

Valencia owes its prosperity, even its very existence, to an immense natural garden, the *huerta*. The *huerta* depends for its sustenance on water – water that cannot be bought or sold, but which is distributed by an extraordinary irrigation network and belongs by right to whoever owns the land through which it flows. Over the centuries the allocation of this vital 'manna' has given rise to constant conflict and litigation. The institution of the Water Court was created in the Arab period. There is no official pomp, no complex rules of procedure, no bureaucracy: justice is verbal, autonomous and immediate. The plaintiff himself pleads his case to the eight judges who represent the eight great irrigation canals of the *huerta*. The Court listens, deliberates and gives its verdict; its decisions, which are not subject to appeal, are applied without delay and fines are paid at once. No justice could be swifter, more effective or more respected. The eight judges are simple peasants elected by their fellow-peasants for their wisdom and their long experience of the most important problem of the *huerta*.

The land is generous. Vast fields of orange-trees and other fruit-trees, melons, market-garden crops, rice and tobacco thrive in this garden blessed by the gods. Twenty million orange-trees provide one of Spain's chief exports (three-quarters of the harvest is sent abroad). The population, equal in density to that of the valleys of the Nile and the Ganges, works continuously from one end of the year to the other, from sunrise to dusk.

Valencia – the Water Court

Peñíscola

No village in Spain belongs to the sea more naturally than **Peñíscola**, built on a rocky peninsula linked to the mainland by a narrow tongue of sand. Peñíscola lives off the sea; the men go fishing, while the women sell the fish and mend the nets. Young people, however, are leaving the village in increasing numbers to seek more secure and remunerative work.

A fortified village, Peñíscola clings to the rock and its narrow streets climb up the slope to the battlemented castle. It was in this castle, at the beginning of the fourteenth century, that the anti-pope Benedict XIII took refuge in his fierce struggle to defend his rights against the Crown and the Holy See. During the War of Independence against Napoleon, Peñíscola endured a siege of eleven days. One would never suspect that this pleasant little fishing village had such a glorious past. . . . .

Peñíscola

Tarragona — the aqueduct

Although pillaged by the Barbarians, **Tarragona** is, with Mérida, one of the two Spanish cities richest in Roman remains. Of very ancient origins, Tarragona enjoyed its greatest splendour at the time of the Roman colonization. It was the place of residence of the consuls and praetors, of Augustus, Galba, and Hadrian who suffered an attempt on his life there. It enjoyed all the privileges of Rome: an amphitheatre, temples, palaces and a circus. On an enclosure-wall of Cyclopean masonry, built with huge unsquared blocks and without mortar, the conquerors erected the new city-walls. The **aqueduct**, 'El Puente del Diablo' (The Devil's Bridge), constructed in the reign of Trajan, bears witness to the greatness and the genius of the Roman people. The downfall of the Roman Empire was also to be the downfall of Tarragona, but the marks of its glory have proved imperishable: many of the houses have been built with the stones of the ancient palaces, inscriptions lie embedded in the walls, and excavations are constantly unearthing treasures which are lovingly preserved by the local archaeological museum.

Tarragona suffered numerous invasions and was on several occasions devastated by the Franks, then by the Moors in the eighth century.

The construction of the **cathedral** – on the site of a mosque, like so many Spanish cathedrals – began at a time when the city was threatened by a new Arab offensive. Its Romanesque apse resembles a fortress. In the thirteenth century the Early Gothic style predominated, in its purest form, to be followed by the Lancet, Flamboyant, Plateresque and Churrigueresque styles. After journeying through Spain, the traveller will not be surprised by such a mixture of styles and their originality cannot be questioned.

Tarragona — the cathedral

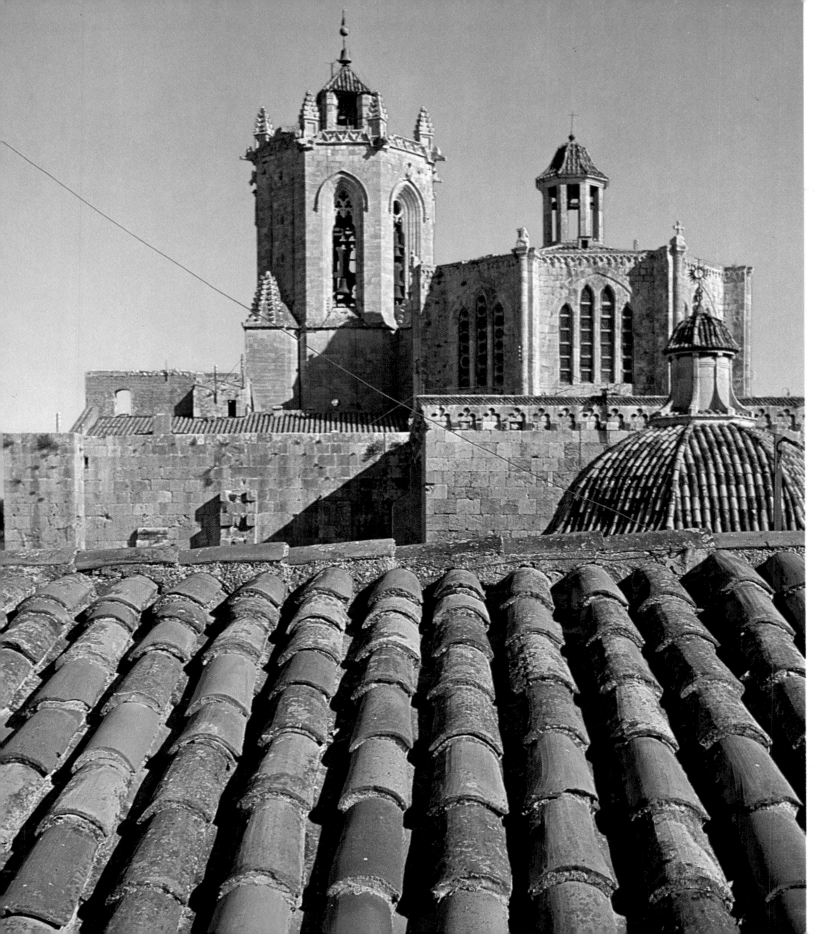

8

FROM BARCELONA TO PORT BOU

Barcelona — Tibidabo

The air that one breathes in **Barcelona** is certainly the most European in the whole of Spain. Like Marseilles and Hamburg, this city is a great seaport with a cosmopolitan character. Even more than Madrid, Barcelona corresponds to one's idea of a great city with its busy crowds, its long grey streets, its blocks of concrete and glass, and its rather austere architecture. If you go up to **Tibidabo**, you will have a glimpse of the city through the great whirling wheels of the permanent fair. From the top of the hill of **Montjuich** there is a panoramic view of the city and its harbour.

The activity of Barcelona dates from the nineteenth century and the Industrial Revolution, the effects of which in Spain were restricted to Catalonia and the Basque Country. But the Catalans' desire for independence goes back further, for the County of Barcelona had never quite accepted its annexation to the Spanish Crown. When the Republic was proclaimed in 1931, Catalonia became a state, the Generalitat de Cataluña; after Franco's victory it was again obliged to become part of a unified Spain. The Catalan of today tends to think that the whole country depends for its wealth on his province.

An industrial and commercial city, Barcelona still asserts its individuality and in its streets Catalan is spoken. It has a charm of its own and, although the modern streets are laid out in a rigid network of straight lines that is far from picturesque, they are nonetheless appealing. From the Monumento de Colón you can walk up the Ramblas, an avenue lined with kiosks, café terraces, second-hand bookshops, florists and bird-shops, to the Plaza de Cataluña. To the left of the Ramblas lies the ill-famed and alluring Barrio Chino, and to the right the Barrio Gótico where there are not only Gothic buildings, but also numerous bars, taverns and restaurants.

Barcelona — the harbour seen from Montjuich

Barcelona — the Ramblas

The Ramblas — the flower market

Barcelona — view from Montjuich

Barcelona — the harbour

Barcelona — the market

Barcelona — the market

Barcelona — dancing on the cathedral square

Barcelona – Museum of Ancient Art. *The Christ Pantocrator of San Clemente de Tahull*

The activity of Barcelona extends to the intellectual and artistic domains. This cultural life is part of the Catalan tradition and is far from diminishing today, either in literature (Goytisolo), the theatre (Nuria Espert) or painting (Tapiés, Cuixart, Valbuena, Mensa, Cardona).

In Barcelona there are two art galleries that are unique in the world, the Museum of Ancient Art and the Picasso Museum. The principal attraction of the Museum of Ancient Art is the collection of extraordinary religious paintings of the eleventh and fifteenth centuries, the most precious of which are the Romanesque frescoes from various Romanesque churches in Catalonia. The monks who painted them succeeded in harmonizing Byzantine and Muslim elements in their glorification of the Lord. The **Christ Pantocrator of San Clemente de Tahull**, with the boldness of its lines, its sense of space, its serenity, epitomizes a faith that leaves no room for doubt.

In the Picasso Museum, in addition to many canvases, engravings and lithographs, are exhibited the fifty-eight paintings called **Las Meninas** (*The Maids of Honour*) which the artist began in 1957. In his search for shape, substance and line, Picasso has discovered the essential character of the infanta's face, thus reaching beyond the pictorial realism of Velázquez. The same desire for simplification seems to have dominated the composition of the Pantocrator. In 1950, while talking to Sabartés, Picasso suggested the possibility of 'copying' the *Las Meninas* of Velázquez: 'I would certainly have to modify the light, since I would have changed the position of one of the figures. And so, little by little, I would paint *Meninas* that would seem detestable to the professional copier; they would not be those he would think he had seen in Velázquez' painting: they would be "my" *Meninas*.'

Barcelona – Picasso Museum. *Las Meninas*.
Detail: the Infanta Margarita María

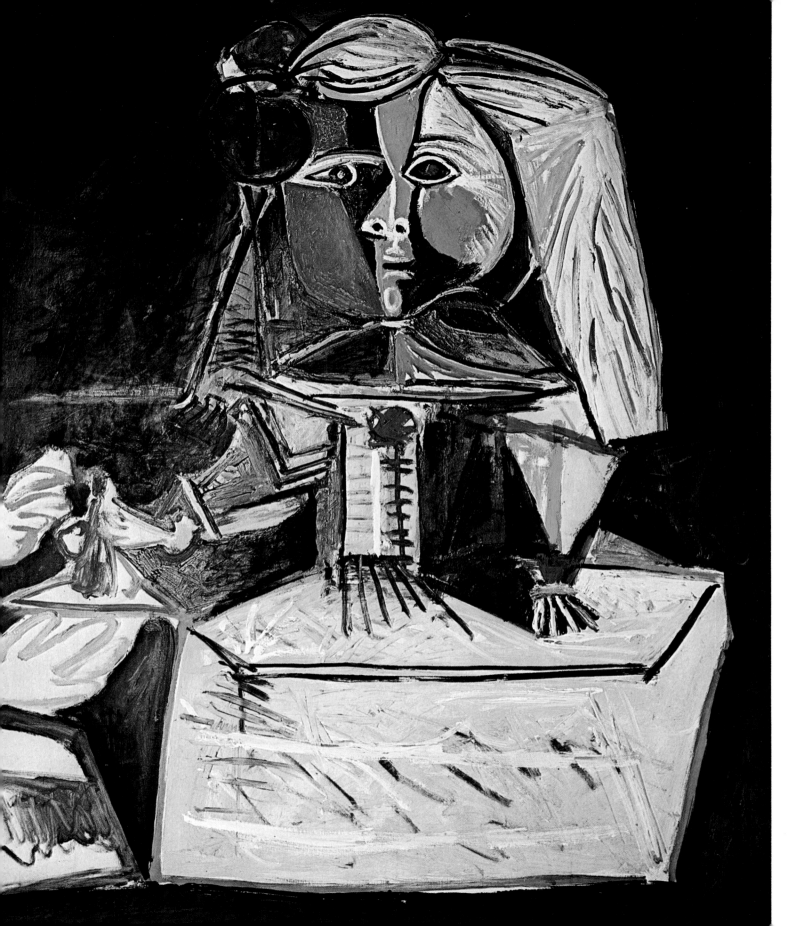

Barcelona — the Sagrada Familia, by Gaudí

Clearly, Gaudí (1852–1926) not only sought to make his buildings blend with their natural setting, but went even further by making vegetation and stone an integral whole. The stone breaks into bud, assuming the form of plants, creepers or seaweed. In his concern with authenticity, Gaudí even introduced casts of plants and animals into his creations.

Barcelona — the Pedrera, by Gaudí

Barcelona possesses a number of his works, which delighted the Surrealists. In the Güell park you can admire the convolutions of his multicoloured ceramic benches. On the Paseo de Gracia you will find the frenzied architecture of the **Pedrera** or Casa Mila, with its waves of stone and balconies decorated with plants.

The **Sagrada Familia** (Church of the Holy Family), begun in 1884 and never completed, is the masterpiece of this singular genius who, in his desire to recreate Gothic art, drew from his imagination a strangely fascinating edifice, like a giant ship wrecked on the bottom of the sea, with its four masts, its broken rigging and its hull overgrown with carnivorous plants.

The Sagrada Familia. Detail of the façade

The Costa Brava

Brava has become a favourite haunt of tourists from every part of the world and the once desolate coastline is now amply populated. At **Tossa de Mar**, San Feliu de Guixols, Palafrugell or Lloret de Mar, the modest villages have been transformed into tourist centres where the sun, the sand and the sea are for sale. Admittedly, the scenery is still the same, but too often it has been disfigured by the indiscriminate building of large modern blocks. There are, however, exceptions. **Cadaqués** is one. This fishing village has been miraculously spared and the new buildings blend discreetly with the countryside. Cadaqués has become as popular as Saint-Tropez and has another cause for pride, for it appears frequently in the paintings of Salvador Dali, who lives not far away at Port Lligat.

The **Costa Brava**, the 'Wild Coast', runs from the north of Barcelona to the frontier. This is a region of stark beauty where the deep blue sea dashes against sheer cliffs and tortuous creeks. Sometimes, in an opening in the rock, one discovers a marvellous little cove with clear waters and a beach of fine sand nestling below the rock-face. The colours here are violent: screes of red rocks, dark caves, white villas, green pines and cork-oaks. In the warm air, cooled by the sea, one breathes the fragrance of lavender, resin and broom.

The road rises high above the peaceful little harbours, wanders among the pine-tracts and the terraced orchards, then plunges down to the glittering sea.

But what is left of that truly 'wild' coast which for hundreds of years was inhabited only by a few fishermen living in simple houses? The Costa

The Costa Brava at Tossa de Mar

Cadaqués

The panorama of **Montserrat** is unforgettable: a chaotic mass of bare reddish sandstone soars upwards forming a fantastic natural rampart. In the moonlight, the grey rocks assume a livid tint and cast sinister shadows. According to a legend, the crevices in the rocks appeared at the moment when Christ died. The monastery contains the miraculous Black Virgin which attracts large numbers of pilgrims every year.

The monastery of **San Pedro de Roda**, also called San Cristóbal after the neighbouring peak, stands in a less forbidding position. To reach this ancient Benedictine monastery, built in the Byzantine Romanesque style, one must clamber up the Sierra de Rosas. Specialists say that this was the first Romanesque edifice to appear in Spain.

The frontier is not far away and so we leave Spain with this last view of San Pedro de Roda, which could well be the beginning of another journey, less ambitious, perhaps, but no less rewarding – a tour of Romanesque Catalonia.

Montserrat — the monastery

The belfry of San Pedro de Roda

The monastery of San Pedro de Roda

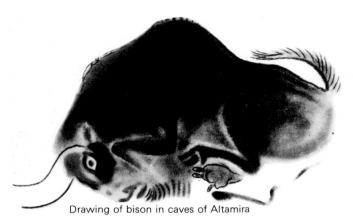
Drawing of bison in caves of Altamira

AN OUTLINE OF SPANISH HISTORY

Santa María de Naranco, near Oviedo

Astrolabe made in 927

Prehistoric Spain

The prehistoric drawings discovered in several regions of Spain show that the peninsula was inhabited from the earliest times. The most famous of these drawings are to be found in the caves of Altamira, near Santillana del Mar, a few miles from Santander.

Spain, the land of invasions

It is generally agreed that the Iberians were the first known inhabitants of the peninsula. They were followed by many different peoples, in particular the Celts in the sixth century BC, the Cretans, the Phoenicians, the Greeks, the Carthaginians and then the Romans, who introduced the Christian religion into Spain. The apostles St Paul and St James went to Spain to preach the Gospel. The Visigoths appeared in Catalonia in 414 and succeeded in creating a unified kingdom around their capital, Toledo.

Divided by a religious conflict, the Visigoth kings weakened their armies in fratricidal wars and as a result the Arabs had little difficulty in overrunning the peninsula.

The Arabs

It took only two years (711–12) for the invasion to be completed, with the exception of the province of Asturias. The Arabs were to remain for eight hundred years in the peninsula. They brought their own civilization to Spain and it was by their efforts that agriculture, industry, the arts, literature and science attained their full glory. Spanish culture was always to bear the imprint of this heritage.

The Reconquest and the Catholic Kings

The time the Reconquest of Spain took varied in different regions from three centuries to eight. The Muslim decline which had

begun in the eleventh century was accelerated by the victory of the Catholic Kings at Las Navas de Tolosa in 1212. Twenty years later, Ferdinand III seized Córdoba, then Murcia, and finally Seville. Only Granada now remained in the hands of the Arabs. But it was not until 1492 that the Catholic Kings, Isabella and Ferdinand of Aragon, obtained the capitulation of the Moorish king Boabdil. There now followed the great period of territorial unity: Castile, Aragon and the kingdom of Granada merged, Castilian became the official language and Catholicism emerged triumphant.

Ferdinand of Aragon and Isabella the Catholic

In the same year that Granada was captured, Christopher Columbus, who had obtained the funds for his expedition from the Catholic Kings, discovered America and the conquest of that vast continent began: Cortez took possession of Mexico and Pizarro occupied Peru.

Christopher Columbus receiving the gifts of the Indian chief, by Th. de Bry

The Habsburgs

Charles I succeeded Ferdinand of Aragon. Elected Emperor of Germany in 1519, as Charles V, he thus became master of the greater part of Europe and of the New World. In his person, the Habsburg family acceded to the Spanish throne which it was to occupy for two hundred years (1517–1700): a century of greatness and a century of decadence.

Charles V, by Titian

During the forty years of his reign Charles V, a man of war and a great politician, succeeded in surmounting all obstacles and in imposing his policy of hegemony. Abdicating in 1556, he left to his son, Philip II, Spain, Italy, the Netherlands, America and North Africa, and to his brother Ferdinand the

Philip II

empire of Germany. Philip II continued his father's policy of hegemony. He became king of England by marrying Mary Tudor. But his religious fanaticism was to lead him into a series of defeats which were the first ominous signs of decadence. This decline became more marked towards the end of the century: wars were being fought incessantly, poverty was widespread, the rural regions were being abandoned, commerce and industry were in jeopardy, and more than forty thousand people were leaving Spain each year for the New World. On the death of Philip II in 1598, Spain remained the leading power in Europe, but Philip III and Philip IV accelerated its decline.

The Bourbons

The accession of Philip V in 1701 marked the arrival of the Bourbon dynasty in Spain. Under the Bourbons, Spanish diplomacy established close links with France. Charles IV entered into an alliance with the Directory and then with Napoleon against Great Britain. The British fleet crushed the Franco-

The Battle of Trafalgar

Spanish fleet at Trafalgar, on 21 October 1805. Napoleon then sent his troops into Spain, compelled Charles IV to abdicate in his favour and then placed his brother Joseph I on the throne.

The War of Independence

The people of Spain soon rose up in rebellion against the invader (Goya depicted the rebellion in *el Dos de Mayo* and *el Tres de Mayo*). The war was a revolution which revealed two Spains: the Spain of Charles IV and his court, who had sold themselves to the foreigner, and the Spain of the people (and of a section of the nobility), which affirmed its dignity and the existence of the Spanish nation.

The Disasters of War, Ya no hay tiempo, by Goya

The Disasters of War, Execution in Spain, by Goya

The armies of Napoleon succumbed in a merciless guerrilla campaign. Ferdinand VII was restored to power in 1812, but betrayed all the hopes that had been placed in him, sweeping the liberals aside and ruling as an absolute monarch. The political troubles provoked by the quarrel between the various monarchist factions led the country to the brink of civil war. These internal difficulties were aggravated by the loss of the greater part of Spain's colonial empire in 1825. After an attempt to establish a Republic in 1873, the monarchy was restored in 1875.

The twentieth century

In 1898 Spain saw the remnants of its colonial empire pass into the hands of the United States. At the beginning of this century Alfonso XIII came to power, but he was not able to stem the internal disorders which eventually led to the dictatorship of General Primo de Rivera in 1923.

Like its predecessor, the Second Republic, proclaimed in 1931, was doomed to failure. Civil war broke out in 1936. At the head of the

Guernica, by Picasso

'National Movement', General Franco, supported by part of the Spanish army, by Moroccan troops and by the Italian and German air forces, made himself master of Spain after thirty months of pitiless warfare. The rest of the story is well known: for more than thirty years the 'Caudillo' has maintained an authoritarian regime in his country.

THE ART AND LITERATURE OF SPAIN

Cervantes

Miguel de Cervantes was born in 1547 at Alcalá de Henares. After an unhappy childhood and a brief course of studies which he never completed, he led a life of adventure. He fought in the battle of Lepanto in which his left forearm was shattered. Captured by the Turks, he then spent five years in the convict prison at Algiers. An affair with an actress resulted in the birth of an illegitimate daughter, Isabel. His marriage to the daughter of a Toledan peasant was a failure. Excommunicated by the canons of Seville, he was arrested four times within ten years. At the age of fifty-seven he was accused of murder but later declared innocent.

Don Quixote and Sancho Panza, by Daumier

Throughout his life Cervantes was constantly becoming entangled with the law. His career as a writer brought him no consolation, for his plays proved unsuccessful. Whatever he did, fate seemed to be against him. The first editions of *Don Quixote* were followed by pirated editions. Misfortune struck again: a year before the second part of this vast fresco of Spanish life appeared, an impostor by the name of Avellaneda published a sequel to *Don Quixote*. In spite of everything, Cervantes' supreme stoicism enabled him to survive these tribulations. He died as he had lived, in 1616, unaware that by writing *Don Quixote* he had joined the ranks of the immortals.

Góngora

Don Luis de Góngora was born in Córdoba in 1561. He completed his studies at the university of Salamanca and then returned to his native city. He decided to enter the Church and was made a prebendary of Córdoba cathedral, but his duties did not prevent him from enjoying a social life. He wrote very little. Like Cervantes, he did not become conscious of his mission as a poet until near the end of his life. Appointed personal chaplain to King Philip III, he settled in Madrid, but court life exhausted him. He returned once more to Córdoba, where he died in 1627.

Illustration for a collection
of Góngora's poems, by Picasso

At the time of their publication the *Fábula de Polifemo y Galatea* and *Soledades,* now regarded as masterpieces, provoked one of the most violent literary controversies of the seventeenth century. It was not until the end of the nineteenth century that Góngora's poetry was fully rehabilitated, largely by the efforts of Verlaine and the Spanish modernists. Since then, the critical studies of Dámaso Alonso and the revaluation of Baroque poetry in general have enabled a wide reading public to recognize his work as one of the highest peaks of Spanish poetry.

Lope de Vega

Born into a modest family in Madrid in 1562, Lope de Vega was educated by the Theatine monks and then at Alcalá. An extraordinarily precocious child, he wrote his first play at the age of thirteen.

His passionate character involved him in a succession of emotional adventures which continued until his death in 1635. His first love resulted in exile in Valencia. After the death of his wife, Isabel de Urbina, he married Juana de Guardo. On the deaths of his second wife and his son, Carlos Felix, he suffered a grave spiritual crisis. He was ordained a priest at the age of fifty-two, but shortly afterwards he met the beautiful actress Marta de Nevares.

His amorous adventures did not prevent Lope de Vega from becoming the most prolific author in Spanish literature, and perhaps even in world literature. His friend Perez de Montalban claimed that he wrote eighteen hundred plays and some four hundred *autos sacramentales.* Among his best-known plays are *Fuenteovejuna, Peribáñez* and *El Caballero de Olmedo.*

'In its universal significance,' wrote Charles V. Aubrun in his history of the Spanish theatre, 'the dramatic work of Lope de Vega can be compared only with Cervantes' *Don Quixote.* One founded the modern European theatre, the other the modern European novel.'

Quevedo

Francisco de Quevedo y Villegas was born in Madrid in 1580. After his early schooling with the Jesuits, he studied classical and modern languages at Alcalá and theology at Valladolid. He then accompanied his friend the Duke of Osuna to Sicily, becoming one of the duke's administrators when the latter was appointed viceroy of Naples. Quevedo accomplished several hazardous diplomatic missions and on one occasion had to flee to Venice disguised as a beggar in order to escape death.

Quevedo

Once Osuna had been dismissed, Quevedo was condemned to exile. He returned to the Spanish court after the death of Philip III. At the age of fifty-four he married a widow whom he left shortly afterwards. He died at Villanueva de los Infantes in 1645.

Quevedo's literary activity covered a variety of genres. His poetic work, published after his death under the titles *El Parnaso español* (1648) and *Las Tres Ultimas Musas*, can be divided into two parts: on the one hand, poems with ascetic and religious themes, grave in tone and clearly didactic in intention; and on the other, poems conceived purely as literary exercises with amorous or humorous subjects, including sonnets of sumptuous artificiality in which Quevedo emulates Góngora. He also wrote political and didactic treatises, the most brilliant of which is undoubtedly *La hora de todos* (1636), written at the height of his genius and described by one critic as his 'Grand Testament'. Quevedo's most widely known work is the picaresque novel *El Buscón*.

Calderón

Pedro Calderón de la Barca was born in Madrid in 1600. His studies at the Imperial Jesuit College, at Alcalá and at Salamanca

Calderón

gave him a solid theological training, but his passion for the theatre soon gained the upper hand. The author of *El Alcalde de Zalamea* settled in Madrid, where he soon became the court's favourite dramatist. The life of Calderón de la Barca offers a profound contrast with that of Lope de Vega: devoted to a scrupulously detailed treatment of the dramatic genre, it was to be dominated by meditation and study. Ordained a priest at the age of fifty, Calderón served as chaplain to the 'New Kings' at Toledo and was then appointed personal chaplain to the king, returning to

Madrid where he remained until his death in 1681.

The philosophical element plays an important part in Calderón's plays. The action is often subordinated to ideas and the characters are then merely symbols of abstract concepts. *La Vida es Sueño* (written in 1635) is generally considered to be his masterpiece. Indeed, some critics regard this play as one of the peaks in the European Baroque theatre.

In addition to his philosophical plays, Calderón wrote dramas about honour (*El Alcalde de Zalamea, El Médico de su honra*), the lives of saints (*El Magico prodigioso*) and mythological subjects taken from legend.

El Greco

Born in 1540 in a village near Candia in Crete, El Greco brought to Spanish art both an Oriental aesthetic creed and Venetian influences. Although practically nothing of his sculpture has survived, his evolution as a painter in Spain can be followed from the *Adoration of the Shepherds* (1578). Most of his works are now either in Toledo, where he settled, or in Madrid. The gallery in Barcelona has a painting dating from his Italian period.

The Baptism of Christ, by El Greco. Detail

His first great Spanish canvas was the *Espolio*, which can be seen in Toledo cathedral. It was in 1583 that he asserted his genius with *The Burial of the Count of Orgaz* (church of Santo Tomé in Toledo).

From 1599 onwards El Greco painted his figures with the elongated bodies for which he is famous (*The Crucifixion, The Baptism of Christ, The Resurrection* and *The Descent of the Holy Spirit*, exhibited at the Prado Museum in Madrid).

El Greco was a visionary of genius. His whole work foreshadowed that of artists such as Cézanne and Van Gogh. He died at Toledo in 1614.

Velázquez

Velázquez was born in 1599. Like all artists of his generation, he began by painting scenes of popular life in the manner of Caravaggio. His religious paintings, with the exception of *The Coronation of the Virgin, Christ on the Cross, Christ at the Pillar* and *St Anthony Abbot and St Paul the Hermit,* also belong to his first period.

At the age of twenty-three he was invited to the court of Philip IV, who had just ascended the throne and whose close friend Velázquez was soon to become. Another important event in the artist's life was his meeting with Rubens in 1628, as a result of which he decided to go to Italy. Twenty years later he revisited Rome and painted a portrait of Pope Innocent X who, as a mark of his esteem, awarded Velázquez a gold chain and a medal bearing his effigy.

In 1657, three years before his death, Velázquez painted *The Tapestry Weavers* which is generally regarded as a masterpiece in the same class as *The Surrender of Breda* and the famous *Las Meninas (The Maids of Honour).*

Goya

Francisco Goya was born on 30 March 1746 at Fuendetodos, a small village in the province of Saragossa. At an early age he began to study painting at the studio of José Luzán. One of his first love-affairs led to his being obliged to leave Saragossa for Madrid. In the capital he met a leading court painter, Mengs, but the young man found himself clashing with the prevailing forces of academicism and obtained only mediocre results in his examinations.

In 1774 Goya married the sister of Francisco Bayeu, who belonged to a great Spanish family and introduced him to the court. This marriage enabled him to enter the royal tapestry factory, where he worked for five years. In 1783 the Count of Floridablanca commissioned him to paint his portrait. Immediately, Goya became the court's favourite painter. But in 1792 an illness left him deaf. Despite success and wealth, the artist's infirmity completely undermined his character and it was at this time that he painted *Los Caprichos.* His wife died in 1812 and Goya then completed two of his most celebrated works: *The Charge of the Mamelukes at the Puerta del Sol* and *The Shootings of May 3.* In 1814 he bought him-

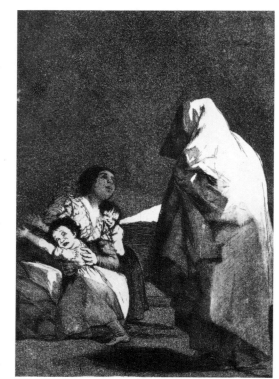
Que viene el Coco, Caprice No. 3, by Goya

self a house beside the Manzanares which soon came to be known as the 'House of the Deaf Man'. He withdrew more and more into himself and devoted his attention to his 'black' paintings, a series of phantasmagorical visions, dark and terrible. Ten years later he left Spain and settled in Bordeaux. A few days after receiving a letter from his son Francis Xavier, announcing that he would shortly be visiting his father, Goya was again struck by illness and died on 16 April 1828.

Jiménez

Juan Ramón Jiménez was born in Moguer, in the province of Huelva, in 1881. At the age of nineteen he left his native village for Madrid. A series of nervous crises made it necessary for him to stay for long periods in sanatoriums in the capital and in the south of France. From 1905 to 1911 he lived once again at Moguer and then returned to Madrid, where he remained for twenty-five years. In 1906 he married Zenobi Camprubi. When the Civil War broke out he emigrated to South America. He died in Puerto Rico in 1958.

After an initial phase of modernist inspiration, Juan Ramón Jiménez began to write highly original poetry which first appeared in *Diario de un poeta recién casado* (1916). In his subsequent work he was concerned only

with perfecting this new style. Among his last volumes published in Latin America were *La Estación total* (1946) and *Animal de fondo* (1949).

Juan Ramón Jiménez exercised a powerful influence on the generation of 1927 and, in particular, on García Lorca. In 1956 the poet, also the author of the world-famous *Platero y yo,* was awarded the Nobel Prize for Literature.

García Lorca

Of all Spanish writers Federico García Lorca is probably the best-known outside Spain. Born in 1898 at Fuentevaqueros, a village in the province of Granada, he studied literature before obtaining a degree in law. From 1919 he lived in Madrid. In 1929 he visited the United States, Canada and Cuba. On returning to Spain, he founded the university theatre known as 'La Barraca' which he directed in partnership with Eduardo Ugarte and for which he adapted Lope de Vega's *Fuenteovejuna* and *La Dama boba,* Tirso de Molina's *El Burlador de Sevilla* and Calderón de la Barca's *La Vida es Sueño.*

His first success as a playwright came in 1927 with *María Pineda,* a triumph that was to be confirmed with *La Zapatera prodigiosa, Bodas de sangre, Yerma* and *La Casa de Bernarda Alba.*

Federico García Lorca published his first collection of poems in 1921. But it was not until the *Romancero gitano* (1928) and the *Poema del cante jondo,* both based on Andalusian folklore, that he succeeded in freeing himself from the powerful influence of

Bodas de sangre, by Federico García Lorca, at the Vieux-Colombier, Paris, in 1963

Juan Ramón Jiménez and finding his own style.

The *Ode to Walt Whitman* (1933) and the *Llanto por Ignacio Sánchez Mejías* (1935) were the poet's last two published volumes before he was shot by the Francoists in 1936.

Buñuel

Luis Buñuel, the eldest of a family of seven children, was born in 1900. He was educated

A scene from Buñuel's *Un Chien Andalou*

A scene from Buñuel's *Viridiana*

by the Jesuits, and completed his studies at the university of Madrid, where he met José Ortega y Gasset, Ramón Gómez de la Serna and the poet Rafael Alberti, and at the same time strengthened his friendships with Salvador Dalí and Federico García Lorca. In 1920 he founded the first film club in Spain.

Buñuel went to Paris in 1925 with the intention of establishing himself in film-making circles. In 1928 he made *Un Chien Andalou*, hailed as a masterpiece by the Surrealists, in 1930 *L'Age d'Or* and in 1932 *Las Hurdes* (*Land without Bread*). After a long eclipse of some fifteen years he made a series of films in Mexico which were rather mediocre except for *Los Olvidados* (1950) and *Nazarín* (1958). Buñuel returned to Spain in 1961 to shoot *Viridiana*. One masterpiece followed another, from *El Angel Exterminador* (1961–62) and *Le Journal d'une femme de chambre*, with Jeanne Moreau in the principal role, to his most recent films, *Belle de Jour* and *La Voie Lactée*. Luis Buñuel is now one of the most revered figures in the art of the cinema.

Picasso

Pablo Picasso was born in Barcelona in 1881. He sketched his first picture at the age of eight and when he was twelve years old claimed that he could already draw as well as Raphaël. He passed the examinations at the art schools of Barcelona and Madrid with disconcerting ease. Although a brilliant academic career lay ahead of him, he felt too cramped in the Spanish artistic circles of the time and seized the first opportunity to escape: the Paris Exhibition of 1900.

Some biographers have divided Picasso's production into periods corresponding with the various amorous episodes of his life – his encounters with Fernande Olivier in 1905, Marcelle Humbert in 1912, Olga Khoklova whom he married in 1918, Marie-Thérèse Walter in 1931, Dora Maar in 1936, Françoise Gilot in 1946 and Jacqueline Roque in 1954 – and it is true that certain rather striking coincidences can be discerned.

Picasso has explored almost every possibility: in turn he has been Nabi, Fauve, Cubist, Constructivist, Abstract, Naïf, Surrealist and Expressionist. A tireless creator, he has always been ahead of his time. On the occasion of his ninetieth birthday the French State accorded him an unprecedented honour by allowing his works to be exhibited in the Louvre during his lifetime.

Las Meninas, by Picasso

TOURIST ITINERARIES AND SUGGESTIONS

To see the whole of Spain in a limited time is clearly impossible. The tourist is advised to plan his journey according to his own personal tastes and preferences, even if this means not seeing everything and saving something for the next visit – for anyone who takes a liking to Spain always returns. The tour described in this book will take at least three weeks, unless the traveller is going to turn a holiday into a marathon race!

1. From the frontier to Madrid

Allow at least three or four days for travelling, seeing the countryside and visiting the cities. Remember that Old Castile is the heart of Spain.

Burgos: one day. Valladolid and Salamanca: one day. Avila and Segovia: one day.

2. Madrid

Three to five days, especially if you wish to explore the Prado and the other museums. For long journeys in Madrid you can take the underground, a double-decker bus or, of course, your own car; but the taxis are strongly recommended, as they are always more convenient in a strange city and are not very expensive.

In Chapter 2 it has been suggested that a tour of the city be divided into historical zones: modern Madrid, old Madrid (preferably on a Sunday), and the museums. But, obviously, you can visit the different parts of the city at random, according to your own particular fancies.

Make sure that you try some *callos a la madrilena* (tripe).

From Madrid you should go to see the Escorial; after visiting the monastery you can take a short stroll through the cool, shady village.

3. Toledo

At least one day. In the evening, visitors are offered a guided tour with illuminations and the old buildings are shown to magnificent effect. Toledo is a small city, so it should be seen on foot; you can buy some souvenirs of chased gold or a replica of the sword of El Cid.

4. Córdoba

Two days. Allow one whole day for the mosque and the surrounding Jewish and Arab quarters. Here you will find a great many craft shops where it is quite normal to bargain when buying (e.g. a bookbinding of local embossed leather).

You can devote your second day to the modern city, its Christian architecture and the immediate environs of Córdoba.

A flower-seller

5. Seville

Three days if you wish to stroll at leisure between visits to places of interest. The first day can be spent visiting the Calle de las Sierpes, Ayuntamiento, the cathedral and the Giralda (go up the inside staircase for a panorama of the city), the Alcázar and the Barrio de Santa Cruz.

On the second day you can visit the Museum of Fine Arts where the major works of Murillo, Zurbarán and Valdés Leal are exhibited; the churches of San Lorenzo, San Gil and Santa Marina; the convent of Santa Clara and the monastery of San Clemente; the Casa del Duque de Alba and the Casa de

Seville – the Plaza de España

Seville – the Plaza de España

Pilatos (in the Mudejar style; according to a legend, this is a reproduction of Pilate's house in Jerusalem).

On the third day you can see the Hospital de la Caridad, the Torre del Oro, the María Luisa park and Triana. If possible you should also go to see the ruins of the ancient city of Itálica (about ten kilometres from Seville).

Remember to see a bullfight (*corrida*). The mantillas in Seville are very beautiful and the cafés are very pleasant.

Environs of Seville: one day.

6. Granada

Three days. You should make a point of strolling round Granada in the evening, when the city is full of the fragrance of jasmin (which can be bought for a few pesetas). At the Alcaicería you can buy a variety of articles inlaid with Arab geometric motifs.

First you can visit the Alhambra and the Generalife.

On the second day you can see the cathedral, the Capilla Real and the church of San Jerónimo, and go for a walk along the Genil.

The third day can be spent visiting the Carthusian monastery, the Paseo del Triunfo, the Albaicín and the Sacromonte (preferably in the evening, so that you can enjoy the gipsy entertainments).

Environs of Granada: one day or more. You can choose between the cool air of the mountains and a well-earned rest by the sea.

7. From Granada to Barcelona

The journey from Granada to Murcia takes a whole day and is likely to be very hot. Stop at Elche, where you can spend a quiet night (unless you prefer the bustle of Alicante).

Valencia is worth a whole day, but you should at least have a meal there and try the incomparable *paella* in a restaurant on the Saler beach. If you are in Valencia on a Thursday you can watch the meeting of the Water Court.

From Valencia to Barcelona: one or two days.

8. Barcelona

At least three days. You should see the Barrio Gótico on foot, for this district of Barcelona offers one delight after another (cathedral, Disputación Provincial, Plaza del Rey, town hall).

On the second day you can go to the Museum of Modern Art, the Ramblas, the modern city, the Museum of Ancient Art and, if you have time, the Tibidabo.

Barcelona – the Sagrada Familia

On the third day you can visit the harbour, the Picasso Museum, Montjuich, the Sagrada Familia, the Güell park and the Barrio Chino.

Try some shellfish at the 'Barceloneta', at the end of the harbour. Ask for a *zarzuela* (a selection of fish and shellfish grilled on the *parrilla*.)

Luis López Alvarez, born in 1930. The holder of diplomas in political science and journalism. He founded the Institute of Congolese Studies in Brazzaville. He has published five collections of poems, an essay entitled *Croissance économique et originalité nationale en Espagne* (P.U.F.) and a book on the Congo, *Lumumba ou l'Afrique frustrée*. He is at present in charge of a department of Unesco.

Madrid

'One cannot stay in Madrid without a visit to the Prado. Some lovers of art remain in the Spanish capital for several days with the sole purpose of going through its rooms systematically. But Madrid has other riches to offer in museums that are less famous but nonetheless worthy of interest.

'According to his own fancies, the visitor can see in turn the Lázaro Galdiano Museum, which contains nearly nine thousand exhibits, including pictures by some of the great masters of world painting; the Romantic Museum, the atmosphere of which is indicated by its very name; the Army Museum, rich in historical memories; and the Valencia Institute of Don Juan, a museum of the decorative arts which has some unique collections of pottery.

'If you do not have much time to spare and your head is spinning after a visit to the Prado, instead of following the main thoroughfares – José Antonio, Alcalá – with their cosmopolitan shop-windows, you should seek a more authentic Madrid. All you need

to do is to go along Calle del Prado, a street where, although it has no particular character of its own, you can browse round the antique-shops. If you have a taste for literature, you can have a look at No. 21, the famous Ateneo. This literary club was the scene of the great intellectual debates that took place in the years before the Civil War. The Ateneo has undergone many changes since then, but the entrance-hall still has the same furniture and the same old-fashioned charm.

'Calle del Prado runs into Plaza Santa Ana, where suddenly you find yourself at the centre of a district enlivened by the comings and goings of the people of Madrid. Sit on a bench and take in all the delightful details of the scene. On the square stands the Spanish Theatre and, at No. 9, a club much frequented by young people, where the singer Ismael appears (after beginning his career in France, Ismael has now found popularity in Spain).

'The young matadors come to Madrid every year to try to gain their "doctorate" in the art of bullfighting. If you find yourself in Madrid towards the end of the morning, on a day when bullfights are being held, you will find in Calle de la Cruz or Calle de la Victoria, near the Plaza Santa Ana, the special atmosphere which always precedes the *corrida*: the *aficionados* queue for tickets, others offer them for resale (sometimes at exorbitant prices), retired bullfighters wander about in search of employment, and the apprentice *toreros* try to make the acquaintance of some *novillero* who has already established himself in the ring and who may be found in one of the innumerable bars of the district, his shirt buttoned up to the collar and his tie fastened round his waist. Here you will be able to enjoy a tasty lunch and your only problem will be an embarrassment of choice.'   L.L. A.

Francisco Curto. Actor, dancer and drama producer.

Córdoba

'One should visit Córdoba in the spring. The city is then a gigantic garden. Its lanes with their evocative names (de las Flores, de los Rincones de Oro, de los Siete Infantes de Lara, de la Hoguera) invite you to stroll along them. Whether you like it or not, you will be bewitched by the play of colours, the golds, ochres, reds and browns contrasting with the immaculate blue of the sky and the sparkling white of the façades. A garden born of a multitude of gardens, Córdoba, like its Andalusian rivals, has its own unique perfume. Through the iron railings you can admire the arrogant jets of water surrounded by a mass of flowers and greenery. As in certain quarters of Seville, the houses of Córdoba are piled up round their patios, like the mud which envelops the diamond. The sudden appearance of a square will briefly interrupt your wanderings through the maze of lanes (be sure you do not miss the Plaza del Potro, which still has its sixteenth-century fountain and the tavern mentioned by Cervantes).

'No visitor to Córdoba should miss the Mezquita, the old Moorish mosque which was second only to the mosque at Mecca and which for many is in itself worth the journey to Córdoba. It is true that, as far as old buildings are concerned, this city cannot offer the same rich variety as Seville or Granada. It is also true that the climate here is more exhausting, especially in summer. But one cannot help being struck by the silence of the city, its mystery and its charm. There are a great many excursions that can be made from Córdoba. Ten kilometres away lie the ruins of Medina Az-Zahara, the finest existing remains of Arab palace architecture (a bus service is provided). Twenty kilometres from Córdoba is the castle of Almodóvar del Río, built by the Moors and fortified by King Don Pedro. You should also visit Las Ermitas de Córdoba, seven kilometres to the north-west of the city. If you like Spanish wines, do not forget to stop at the cellars of Moriles and Montilla. But if you are pressed for time, do not worry, as you will certainly be able to taste these wines in any of the city's restaurants, where you should also try three specialcialities of the province: *el ajo molinero, la sopa de maimones* and *las patatas en ajopollo*.

'I have told you almost nothing about my city. But how could it be otherwise? Words are often inadequate. Come to Córdoba and stay here for a few days, a week, or even for the whole of your holiday. When you leave, I am sure that you will be as incapable as myself of explaining what it is that has captivated you here. Half-way between the past and the future, a certain charm perhaps . . . simply that.'
F. C.

Jean-Michel Fossey. Once lived in Seville, which has made an unforgettable impression on him; he goes back to the city whenever he can. A journalist and writer, he has published a volume of poetry entitled *la Mémoire immédiate*.

Seville

'"Seville for wounding the spirit", said Federico García Lorca, and I proved this to myself on arriving in the city. Indeed, nothing could be more painful and, at the same time, more agreeable than to lose oneself in the lanes of the Santa Cruz quarter the heart of Seville and of Andalusia. I do not know what to advise you to see first. It would probably be wiser to suggest that you stroll along the streets at random, losing yourself among them, breathing their perfume, gazing at the sky and allowing yourself to become intoxicated, for Seville, as the poet Luis Cernuda so rightly said, is like no other city in the world. But you will no doubt be pressed for time like most tourists, and so I offer the following suggestions. After exploring the Santa Cruz quarter (Calle de la Pimienta and Calle del Agua, Santa Marta, Doña Elvira and Santa Cruz squares), go to the Alcázar. A large part of the walls and towers of the enclosure, the Puerta del León and the arcades of the Patio del Yeso have survived the ravages of time. Walk through its gardens (Seville is the city of gardens). To the east of the Alcázar lie the Murillo gardens, which extend as far as the Paseo de Catalina de Ribera. Retracing your steps, you can then go along Calle San Fernando and Avenida Sanjurjo, which comes out near the Tower of Gold, so named by the Arabs. The tower stands beside the Guadalquivir and houses the Naval Museum, where the exhibits include models, pictures, engravings, nautical maps, and so on.

'As you leave the Tower of Gold you can choose whether to cross the river and visit the Triana district, or to go along the Hospital de la Caridad as far as the cathedral. I strongly recommend that you opt for the latter, since the gipsies deserted Triana a long time ago and this district no longer offers any special attraction (nowadays it is no different from any other popular quarter). There are so many old buildings to be seen in Seville: the cathedral, the Giralda (the minaret of the old mosque, erected in the twelfth century). . . . But looking at these architectural monuments is only one of the reasons that tourists are tempted to prolong their stay in this city, for Seville has another pleasure to offer; it has the best night life of any city in Spain. If you come out of season you will have no difficulty in making the acquaintance of native Sevillians (for heaven's sake avoid the summer months and the Holy Week festivals, unless you have been conditioned to such a point that you can enjoy only the Spain of operetta-style bullfighters and gipsy dancers who seem to have been mass-produced on a factory conveyor-belt). The Andalusians have preserved something quite rare in Europe, a relish for conviviality, in spite of their poverty – or perhaps because of it. In their company you will be able to try some of the excellent local wines (from Villanueva de Ariscal, Pilas or Lebrija), not forgetting those from Jerez de la Frontera or the port of Santa María. You will not need a guide for pleasures of this kind and so I leave you in good company: just remember that everything will depend on you.'
J.-M. F.

José María Alfonso Sánchez, born in Granada in 1927. A journalist and writer, he has published two volumes of poetry: *Amor es muerte* and *Primo Tempo*.

Granada

'"A closed paradise . . . an open garden", in the words of Pedro Soto de Rojas. Three roads lead to Granada: the north road, if you come from Baza (remember to visit the ancient palace of Abrantes) and Guadix; the west road; or the south road, which, from Lanjarón, winds its way through the valley of Lecrín. If possible, you should enter the city through one of the ancient gates. Granada, beautiful, obscure and remote, may allow you to discover her secrets. Begin with a visit to the church of San Jerónimo in Calle San Juan de Dios, where the remains of the Gran Capitán (Captain Gonzalo de Córdoba) are preserved. On leaving the church, pause briefly at the Royal Hospital and then take Calle Real de Cartuja, allowing time to stroll at your leisure, for this is one of the pleasures of a visit to Granada. At the Carthusian monastery (*cartuja*) you will find the Baroque splendour of Hurtado Izquierdo. The monastery deserves a special mention: its sacristy has been called the Christian Alhambra because of the beauty of its plaster decoration. Return to the city-centre along Calle Elvira; before you come to the end of this street turn right and you will come into the Gran Vía. Visit the Chapel Royal which is built on to the cathedral; the chapel was erected by Enrique Egas to serve as a tomb for the Catholic Kings, whose remains have rested here since 1521. Not far from the cathedral are the Alcaicería, formerly the Moorish cloth market and now Granada's craft market, and the Corral del Carbón (an Arab hostelry).

'Make your way into the maze of lanes of the Albaicín and look for the tower of San José, originally the minaret of the Almora-Bitín mosque. Wander slowly through the lanes and pause to enjoy the views of the magnificent Alhambra which appear from time to time. When you come into the Plaza San Miguel, you can relax in one of the numerous taverns (*tascas*) and drink some of the local wine, before continuing your walk to the palace of Daralhorra and the balcony of San Nicolás, a splendid viewpoint looking out on to the Alhambra. Then go back to Plaza Nueva. Climbing the hill of Gomérez, you will come to the Alhambra wood, which did not exist in the time of the Moors. This place was then a fortified city. Go through the Justice Gate and make your way up to the Vega Tower. If you do this on New Year's Day in the company of the person you love and if you are the first ones to touch the bell of the tower, you will be married during the year! The view from the top of the tower is marvellous in whatever direction you look. You can see the Sierra Nevada, the city, the Sierra Elvira, the Generalife and the Alhambra itself. And in the Alhambra I will now leave you to lose yourself at your leisure.'

J.M.A.S.

Antonio Gálvez, born in Barcelona. Eric Losfeld has recently published his *Buñuel*, which received the unanimous praise of critics. He is writing a book about the leading Latin American authors and also has articles published in various Spanish and Latin American journals.

Barcelona

'A visit to the Barrio Chino is well worthwhile. Go and dine at the "Portalón". You will have no difficulty in finding this tavern. When you reach the Liceo theatre in the Ramblas, take Calle Boquerías and then turn left into Calle Baños Nuevos. The "Portalón" is about two hundred yards along this street. On the way you can look in the windows of the antique-shops, which are very numerous in this area (especially in Calle Baños Nuevos, Calle de la Paja and Calle San Severo).

'With a bit of luck you will find at the "Portalón" the *cinéaste* José María Nunes, the Argentinian writer Nestor Sánchez, the painter Pedro Pruna and the critic Manuel Quinto, who will be only too glad to help you discover the marvels of Barcelona. If, however, luck is not on your side and if you want to visit places other than museums and monuments of architecture, you can always follow this itinerary which, if it should prove disappointing, has never yet disappointed me.

'Starting from the harbour and making your way towards Plaza de Cataluña, take the second street on your left and make a brief call at the "Pastis" bar. The paintings of the proprietress' late husband are displayed inside; although of little artistic interest, these portraits of prostitutes are worth seeing. Nearby is a dance hall, the "Cádiz", which has the advantage of not yet having been discovered by tourists. The presence in Barcelona of the sailors of the American fleet adds an extra piquancy to an already highly flavoured city.

'From the Ramblas turn left on to either Calle San Pablo or Calle del Hospital, both of which come out at one end of Calle Robador, a succession of bars and brothels. Two *grises* (policemen) pace up and down continually, but without in any way damaging the street's thriving trade; they are there only to maintain appearances, as prostitution does not officially exist in Spain. Calle Robador is a frontier which most tourists will not want to cross, while for others it is the antechamber of a truly Goyaesque inferno. At all events, it is worth lingering there a while. This cannot be said of Calle San Ramon and Calle Tapias, through which you must pass to reach the Paralelo and which, after a certain hour of the night, give the "Chinese Quarter" its sordid aspect of earlier days, as described so admirably by Jean Genet in his *Journal d'un voleur*. You can end your evening at the "Molino", which offers strip-tease Spanish-style, usually quite amusing though of poor quality. If you are not yet satisfied, return to your starting-point in front of the Liceo theatre. Not far away is Plaza Real where, in both summer and winter, you can enjoy the flamenco dancing and singing at the "Los Tarentos" night-club.'   A. G.

Tauromaquia, by Picasso

Bullfighting

Barbarous, cruel, but also beautiful, the *corrida* is a contest in which man takes pleasure in playing with death, in proving his superiority. In recent years the arrival in Spain of vast numbers of foreign tourists has caused the bullfight to lose much of its original character. It tends nowadays to be regarded more and more as a spectacular show. In the seaside villages bullfights are hastily organized with the sole purpose of satisfying holidaymakers. Nevertheless, the big bullfights are still more or less the same as in earlier days and are worth watching, especially those at Valencia (17, 18 and 19 March), Madrid and Barcelona (during the Easter festivals), on the feast of St Isidore in Madrid (in May), on Corpus Christi in Granada, on the feast of St Firmin in Pamplona (6–12 July), in Barcelona (24–26 September) and in Saragossa (16 October).

The *corridas* take place in the afternoon and always follow the same ritual. Six bulls are killed, having been drawn by lot by three matadors. Each fight, under the direction of a president, lasts twenty minutes.

The proceedings begin with the *paseo* or ceremonial presentation of the *cuadrillas* (the teams of bullfighters): the *alguaciles*, *matadores*, *peones* and arena attendants then salute the president. When the *peones* have tired the bull with a few passes of the cape, the mounted *picadores* harass it with their spears and then the *peones* stick their darts between the bull's shoulders (sometimes the matador himself likes to do this). Then follows the duel proper between the matador and the bull, ending with the stabbing of the animal. According to the degree of bravery shown by the matador, the crowd waves handkerchiefs to ask that he be awarded one ear, both ears, the tail or even a foot of the dead bull; the president will grant or refuse their request as he thinks fit.

Spanish cuisine

In Barcelona you can enjoy some of the most colourful food in Spain. In particular, the authors recommend *escudella i carn d'olla* (Catalan stew), *butifarra con judías* (pork sausage with French beans), *habas estofadas* (braised beans) and *perdices con coles* (partridge with cabbage). With your meal have some *priorato*, *alella*, *perelada* or *villafranca*.

In Madrid you should try the *cocido* (meat and vegetable stew), the *callos a la madrileña* (tripe) and some *serrano* ham. The two local wines are *valdepeñas* and *rioja*. In Andalusia you can try the *gazpacho* (cold soup with raw vegetables – tomatoes, cucumber, etc.). In the harbour towns along the coast have some *chanquetes* and *boquerones* (freshly caught anchovies), which go perfectly with the glass of sherry (*jerez*) that you will drink as an apéritif. The *rabo de toro* (bull's tail) is the local speciality of Córdoba and Seville. In addition to sherry, you will have a wide choice of wines, including *montilla*, *moriles* and *manzanilla*.

As well as the various regional specialities, you must try the *tortilla*, a large peasant omelette with potatoes, onion and *chorizo* (Spanish sausage), at least once during your stay in Spain.

A garlic-seller

CONTENTS

First published in Great Britain by
Kaye & Ward Ltd
21 New Street, London EC2M 4NT
1973

First published in the USA by
Oxford University Press Inc.
200 Madison Avenue, New York N.Y. 10016
1973

ISBN 0 7182 1000 X (Great Britain)
ISBN 0 19 519726 7 (USA)
Library of Congress Catalog Card Number 73-76914 (USA)

All enquiries and requests relevant to this title should
be sent to the publisher, not to the printer.

Printed in Italy by
Arnoldo Mondadori Company Ltd, Milan